BAD MOMMY
BAD WRITER

Writing From Home While
Keeping the Kids Alive

KIM COOPER FINDLING

Paperback ISBN: 978-1-945587-68-9
Library of Congress Control Number: 2021936837

1. Motherhood; 2. Writing; 3. Working from home; 4. Career

Book editing, design & project production: *Dancing Moon Press*
Cover illustration, design & production: *Dancing Moon Press*
Manufactured in the United States of America

Dancing Moon Press
dancingmoonpress.com
Bend, Oregon
Lincoln City, Oregon

DANCING
MOON
PRESS

For Libby and Maris

Forever and always, job number one.

Popcorn

January 2, 2009

I sit down to write my first blog entry. I begin the first sentence. I hear, "Mommy, we want popcorn!" I get up. I pop popcorn.

Never mind that it is 7:43 a.m. and some other mommies might not think popcorn is a breakfast food. I deliver the bowl to the requesting parties. I return to my office. I begin sentence two.

"Mommy, my juice spilled!" I get up. I fetch paper towels to clean up the half-apple juice/half-water mixture which has escaped from the disobedient sippy cup. I replace the sippy cup with a new and hopefully more obedient one.

"Tanks," says one of the two requesting parties. I return to my office. I begin sentence three.

And now, allow me to introduce my children, Chicken Noodle (three going on four) and Chicken Little (almost two): co-conspirators, helpmates and hinderances on my writer's journey, depending on the day.

Also included in the cast of my life is Captain Daddy, but he's not here this morning, which is either a bad thing (if he were here he might possibly play with our chickens and give me some time to write) or a good thing (equally possible is that he would serve as judge and jury to the whole video/popcorn situation).

I predict that in just a moment, Chicken Little will lose interest in *Toy Story* and appear here at my desk, the top of her little blonde curls brushing my elbow. "Up, Mommy," she will say.

I will lift her on to my desk alongside photos and seashells and stickers and to-do lists until she destroys something.

The possibilities here are endless: the phone? The photo of her and Santa? A magazine contract?

Nevertheless that will be my cue to accept defeat for this writing session, having completed a grand total of 200 words—not entirely impressive or terribly impressive depending on how you view the conditions under which they occurred.

This leaves only 2,999,800 to go, according to Ray Bradbury's theory that writing three million words would equate with achieving writing mastery. You've set high standards, Ray, but I'll get there, even if it takes until Chicken Little is in college.

Blooming Eventually

January 11, 2009

Me these days: Mother, wife and writer watching forty climb the front steps like a peddler pushing time, and me with nowhere to hide.

The writer part used to come first, the forty used to be thirty, and marriage and motherhood were abstract activities I thought I'd try someday.

Ah, growing up. If only it was the thrill promised when we were six.

I have written hundreds of articles and essays, many of which have been published. I have written a book, which has not been published. It has been rejected. Repeatedly. Once, not so long ago, I even set the entire five-years-in-the-making-but-horribly-doomed manuscript on fire.

Did that disastrous bonfire stop me on this preposterous quest to publish a book? Why no, it did not. I keep banging away, determined to get this writing thing right eventually. I am persistent. All I want in the whole wide world besides being a good mother is to be an author. No matter how much self-abuse it takes, I will publish some kind of book-like object.

But writing is hard. And the publishing industry is a beast. And I am terrified of exposure, mediocrity, and most of all, failure. And most of my days are spent trapped under a pile of plastic princesses or scraping peanut butter off the wall.

So, the question remains—will I bloom, eventually? Will I molder away like a dud shrub in some forgotten corner of the side yard? Or will I ditch the whole writing thing, adopt a Xanax habit, abandon my own identity and live the rest of my life vicariously through my children?

Hmm, let's find out.

Things I Learned This Week

January 12, 2009

If your child poops on the booth seat in a restaurant, you will feel obliged to leave an extra-large tip.

Happy New You!

January 14, 2009

Last week was Captain Daddy's birthday. Presumably because this day comes on the heels of the holidays, Chicken Little was understandably, adorably confused and spent the day trilling, "Happy New You, Daddy!"

Only a twenty-two-month-old could come up with such a delightful, innovative way to announce the beginning of another personal year.

How many "new yous" are left for Captain Daddy and me, I wonder? Not how many actual birthdays—he is forty-five, I am thirty-eight; let's hope lots. But how many true reinventions of self?

Maybe because I am approaching forty, lately I have been feeling the weight of the doors which have closed behind me; the narrowing of the possibilities which define my current life.

Youth holds such potential. Even if you never do, in the back of your mind you know you could always move to Argentina, quit your job and go to medical school, sell your stuff on the lawn and hitchhike to Europe, join the circus and learn the trapeze.

I never did any of those things in my twenties, by the way; I waitressed, partied and earned two college degrees, neither of which I'm currently using, if you must know.

By choosing other, more conventional things instead (which most of us eventually do)—marriage, parenthood, job, mortgage—those doors begin to close. Simply by growing up, we limit our options.

The trapeze is no longer possible, even as a daydream.

This process is as much reassuring as it is unsettling, which is why some people do it too soon and others never do it at all.

Other advantages of youth are taken from us with no choice at all—beauty, for instance. Oh, the possibilities inherent to beauty, how powerful you were, how quickly you abandoned me. But that is another story.

I don't regret one single thing that has happened to me (well, maybe the loss of beauty, and one or two other things unfit for print), or any of the circumstances that anchor me now. But those closed doors lately linger like ghosts in my mind.

That so many of the Ys in the road I encountered were one-chance-only is only really clear to me now, in hindsight.

What forks in the road remain for me now? Many, I suspect. First there will be the myriad this-or-that decisions to be made in the process of completing the herculean projects of motherhood and marriage. Besides that, I imagine my "new yous" will mostly occur in the arena of the self: in the fine tuning of my days and my work.

This, when you think about it, is pretty damn exciting. Perhaps even more so than the trapeze.

Shitshow with a View

January 17, 2009

Post-bath time the other night, two naked chickens ran wild. Their mother was touring their bedrooms, in search of flannel zip-up pjs. She was in the home stretch, she could see it—the beautiful chickens in bed and her with an episode of *Big Love* streaming on the laptop, a wee dram of vodka, an hour to herself before she, too, collapsed into sleep, in preparation for another day of love and the motherhood-rodeo.

That's about when the chickens decided to tag team the granite-topped table that sits against the wall in the living room.

I returned to see them both dangling from the tall, tippy table with their full, naked weight, wriggling in joy in what appeared to be a pursuit not unlike pole dancing, although much more alarming (as if that were possible).

The table came crashing down on top of their precious, perfect, bare-naked little bodies.

Captain Daddy to the rescue!

Nope.

Let me enlighten you on the irony of being married to a paramedic/firefighter—chances are, when you need him, he'll be off saving other people's lives. Hero to the masses, phantom to me.

Around here, most of the time, Mommy performs her own rescues.

I scanned both babies for obvious injury and found none, but I'd seen that table smash into them, man. Given the time of day, the option of just monitoring them for an hour or so was out. I could not really just stuff them into bed and pour myself a drink without knowing whether or not they had internal injuries just waiting to fester in the night.

I bundled the chickens into their pjs, loaded everyone into the car, and made it to urgent care for last call. On the way, Chicken Noodle ogled the night sky, cooing, "Mommy, the stars! They are so glowy!" (We never go out at night. Night is for sleeping babies and vodka nightcaps.)

The doc looked over my priceless progeny and deemed them perfectly unharmed. We closed down urgent care the way I once shut down bars, last ones out beside the staff.

Back in the car and rolling for home, the canopy of stars glimmered brightly in the winter's night sky. Both of my chickens gazed up contentedly from their car seats, mesmerized, quiet as mice, safe and whole, reminding me once more that every single shitshow has a silver lining.

Late Bloomers

January 19, 2009

Malcolm Gladwell wrote an article titled "Late Bloomers" for *The New Yorker* last year. It was based on work for his book *Outliers* and compared two kinds of creative genius.

He explains that there are two manners of achieving a work of art. In the first, a person sees their project fully formed in their mind and sets forth, often at a young age, to achieve it quickly and entirely.

The other is much more experimental and time consuming. We (yes, this one is me) thrash about, putting together one version and then another of whatever it is we mean to create; we fail, we fling the last draft into a tree, we burn the book, we beat ourselves up, we get a new idea, we try again.

Every time, we are filled with hope that this time we will get it right. Mostly, we don't. We despair. But we can't stop working at it. We keep trying. We throw things at the wall and hope something sticks. And eventually some of us do get it absolutely, gorgeously right.

There is no guarantee I will be one to eventually bloom. It is not a sure thing that my book will be published someday, or that I will publish some other book instead. But Gladwell's article gave me a renewed sense of hope.

It was nice, in the first place, to recognize myself in a methodology occasionally witnessed to produce great art. I thought of myself as simply neurotic, insecure and slightly deranged; well, then, so was Cezanne, and look what he managed to do.

But even more helpful was an understanding of the bottom line when it comes to achieving success as a late bloomer— persistence. All of that trying and flailing takes time, and also, it counts as practice. The key is not giving up (also implied in Ray Bradbury's write-three-million-words-and-gain-mastery theory).

Gladwell's article was also, of course, the inspiration for this blog. I am, hopefully, before your very eyes, blooming eventually.

Deep inside, I believe my book will be published. It might be in ten or twenty years, but someday, I feel it will be published. I believe this partly because I can't stand the thought of it not being published, but also because I know I am self-abusive enough to carry on long past any reason.

Allow me to live long enough, allow me to steal enough hours from my children and husband, allow me to demure from other hobbies I might otherwise take up, like guitar-playing or surfing or scrapbooking (well, probably I'd never take up scrapbooking), and I will produce something worth publishing as a book-like object.

Trust me.

Funny, I Don't Remember That

January 19, 2009

Chicken Noodle: "When I was one, I fell into a swimming pool without a grown-up and sunk to the bottom and lost my breath and had to go to the hospital. I've been meaning to tell you that."

Boomerang

January 22, 2009

After I set fire to the manuscript I'd spent five years writing, I needed something else to do with my restless, relentless pursuit of authordom, so I wrote a children's book.

Twelve weeks ago, I sent out seven queries and manuscripts for that little throw-things-at-the-wall-see-if-they-stick consolation prize project. I think it's safe to say at this point I've gotten all of the responses I am going to get from that effort, which is to say, precisely one.

That lonely reply was a boomerang—what I call the rejections that come back so fast you just know they couldn't possibly have actually made it to New York and back. It was a preprinted form letter, barely a half-sheet of paper, which read something like:

"Dear Author/Illustrator (*because we can't be bothered to distinguish between the two of you*),

We are sorry to tell you that your manuscript doesn't seem right for our list (*because it sucks, or, possibly, because we didn't read it*). We are grateful to you for thinking of us (*really?*) and we wish you the best of luck in finding a publisher (*as long as it's some other sorry bastard*).

Sincerely, Editorial Department (*or more likely some depressed twenty-two-year-old intern who thought she'd made it in the Big Apple until she found herself slaving away twelve hours a day for soup money in a cubicle wearing her roommate's borrowed heels*)."

The sad news is that this crumpled mass-produced rejection letter counts as tremendous feedback compared to the deafening silence from the other six publishers.

I read in *TIME* magazine today that Stephanie Meyer sent out something like nine queries, got three rejections, five non-answers and one interested person. We hear these stories all of the time; they are meant to buoy us, apparently.

I just think it's depressing. Can the publishing world not be bothered to *reject* us in the self-addressed-stamped-envelope *we* supply?

But none of that nasty negativity, now! We shall forge on, in search of an actual human being to one day read our slaved-over words and perhaps even tell us what they thought of them.

Adapt and Overcome!

January 24, 2009

I'm sorry. That was uncalled for. Bad writer.

I've just spent an hour identifying eight new publishers to submit my children's book manuscript to (must get back on the bus!), and am feeling chagrined about my rant of last post. I, and all the other wannabe authors in the world, have been duly warned.

No news is normal news. There are caveats all over the writing world that publishers, when uninterested, will simply not respond. Same for editors and agents. They got shit to do, man, and it isn't responding to everyone they don't want to work with.

It's still a sorry state of affairs, in my opinion. But I recognize that it is much easier (and far less useful) to rant than to simply accept the conditions one must work under and persevere anyway.

"Adapt and overcome!" my wise stepfather has begun to declare at the tiniest sign of challenge. I will submit these next eight and try not to take personally the absolute nothingness that might (or might not! must remain hopeful!) follow.

Better Than an Acceptance Letter

January 25, 2009

Chicken Noodle: "Mommy you are the bestest. You are a good listener. Good job. You get a lollipop."

I'll Take the Frog

January 26, 2009

Yesterday afternoon I stood before a row of humidifiers, trying to make a decision. Would it be the adorable, frog-shaped machine that would make Chicken Little smile, or the practical, cheaper one that would make sense beyond the animal-appliance days of young childhood?

The world swayed and my mind went fuzzy.

Maybe if I hadn't been so tired, I could've performed this simple task.

My day had started at 5:00 a.m. when I loaded a croupy and feverish Chicken Little into the car and drove her to the ER. But really the previous day had never ended. I'd been up most of the night with her vomiting, wheezing, hot little self.

The ER meds had helped, and we'd spent the day since in a dreamy daze. She'd wanted to be held, so the two of us had curled up on the couch with blankets, videos, and several issues of *The New Yorker*.

The day had reminded me of so many similar days before, when she (and her sister before her) was a newborn. When having a small person in my lap meant the phone rang and I didn't answer it; showers were delayed if considered at all; laundry and the dishes languished; nothing was written but maybe a barely sensible email; consciousness swam in and out of focus and bleary-eyed exhaustion became forever correlated with a bliss never known before and never matched again—the utter contentment of holding your own gorgeous child for an entire day; the peacefulness of what it means to finally know the truth of family, and of love.

I reached out with both hands, tucked the frog humidifier under my arm, and headed for home.

Overheard

January 28, 2009

Husband Acquaintance: "It's so frustrating being with the baby. I can't get anything done."
Wife Acquaintance: "Being with the baby is getting something done."

Burn Baby Burn

January 29, 2009

Yeah, so, I set fire to my book last year. Every last page of it, in the brick cavity of an undersized fireplace in an average vacation rental on the McKenzie River, after a minor yet tear-soaked ceremony to bid the whole flipping disaster goodbye.

I did this not because the manuscript was a pile o'crap, although maybe it was. I burned my book because it was consuming me. Four rewrites and five dozen rejections and the thing had taken on a life of its own; its rejection, my own; its subject, my identity.

Have you ever had your life experience rejected by two-sentence emails? It very extremely sucks.

One of us had to go.

The thing about memoir is that it's too easy to take too personally. It is your own life you are putting out there on display and for judgment, after all. Writing about your own life can also make you treat your days like they are part of a Hollywood script.

As I was living, I was thinking about the book constantly. As I went about my business, I'd be compelled to ask myself, "Is this thematically relevant? Is this the climax?"

Finding the ending had become a bit of a quandary because life kept on happening while I was trying to write. Again with the not particularly helpful self-inquiry—"Should I wait another week—will the happy ending show up by then?"

In short, I was trying to cram my life into the formal structure of the novel. This process was eating me alive, not to mention keeping me from enjoying the day-to-day imperfect beauty of my own wacky life rather than trying to turn it into a plot point.

So, I lit fire to the thing. It was instantly, wholly liberating.

But do I really finally believe that this tale doesn't have to be published for it to be a true story? Maybe. We'll see if I'm really capable of putting that story down for good. I still want to figure out that happy ending, I really do, even if it's just for me.

She Used to Say Smart Things

February 1, 2009

Here are some things I say (nearly) every day:

Don't eat the crayons.
Daddy's grumpy.
Who wants to boingy?
It's not okay to show your vagina to the whole world.
Get off of the coffee table.
Don't hit your sister.
Five more minutes.
I love you so much.

cMama Goes Hawaiian

February 3, 2009

Brief status update from Hawaii, where our protagonist has traveled to her mother's house with her eldest child for a bit of R&R.

Interest in creating pithy, fabulously interesting blog post: Very low.

Interest in staring stupidly into the tropical middle distance: Very high.

Favorite part of this vacation so far: Phoning home and finding that the chickens are most interested in talking only to each other. They report on their experiences, whilst apart.

"Hi Boo Boo!" trills Chicken Noodle. "I love you! I had shave ice. Grandma bought me a fairy. Mommy fell off the surfboard. I miss you Boo Boo!"

"Hi. Sis." Chicken Little speaks in her adorable, halting twenty-three-month-old syntax. "Hot. Ducky. Daddy. Tub. Slide. Home."

Thanks, Fred

February 5, 2009

The good news: I did not make a total arse of myself during my first-ever surfing lesson.

The bad news: It was nonetheless clear that I will not be mastering that sport in this lifetime.

Aside from forcing my ridiculously nervous self down to Waikiki and forking out $40 to fling myself into the ocean with only a really gigantic polyurethane board tied to my ankle to save me, I managed to read the entirety of Malcolm Gladwell's *Outliers* on vacation. He has many fascinating things to say about success, mostly converging on the themes of luck and hard work.

The good news *and* the bad news: Luck I can't do much about. Hard work is entirely up to me.

Gladwell describes the 10,000-hour rule, which declares that mastery of any skill can be achieved with the investment of 10,000 hours of good old-fashioned hard work. This implies that, were I to move nearer the ocean and continue to wade into it daily for the next decade or two, I could potentially still become a pretty decent surfer.

However, as I hauled the board up onto the sand three days ago, arms shaking from the effort of one hour's worth of learning something altogether new, it occurred to me that I am already well on my way to 10,000 hours spent writing, and perhaps it is just common sense to apply myself where I have a solid head start.

The very best part? As my surfing instructor, I had expected some local hottie dude: young, muscled, long-haired, full of himself and intimidating as shit.

Instead I got Fred: local, all right—as well as scrawny, wrinkled, balding and sixty-eight years old. SIXTY-EIGHT FREAKING YEARS OLD!

I LOVED Fred. Fred was patient. Fred called me sweetheart, in good way. Fred was so happy to simply be in the water. Fred knew what the heck he was doing. Fred had me standing and surfing within twenty-five minutes.

Fred was the embodiment of the 10,000-hour rule. As a surfer, he was beyond competent, delighted, and happy to share his knowledge.

My new goal: when I am sixty-eight, to be the Fred of writing.

Me, Justified

February 9, 2009

"Explain yourself," my stepfather intoned from the driver's seat as we traveled to the north shore of Oahu. "Justify your existence!"

He snickered wickedly. This is his idea of small talk.

JB is cursed with an existential preoccupation. He takes stock of life regularly—his and everyone else's. What have we accomplished? What will we leave behind? And, after all that, are we *happy*? Have we learned to let go, figured out what matters, mastered a pitch-perfect balance of meaning, occupation and pleasure?

I have this same problem. That's why we get along so well.

Of course, he was only joking about me justifying my existence in a twenty-five-minute car ride. Sort of.

He giggled with delight. "Well?"

What I might have said is that the problem with hard work is that I've never felt like it was the only way to go.

I've done a lot of writing in the past decade but not 10,000 hours worth because I've filled half of those hours with other things—hiking and skiing and camping and reading a novel in the sunshine and drinking beer and learning to play the guitar and napping and loving and running and making money and raising babies and, finally last week, a little surfing.

I've never wanted to spend all of my life working, and I never have. I didn't even figure out I wanted to be a writer until I was thirty. So really, I kind of just got started.

Perhaps at some point justifying my existence will mean learning not to apologize—for unachieved successes or for what was compromised for the sake of happiness.

Alright, Confession

February 10, 2009

Can you keep a secret? You know that book I told you I burned up?

Well, within the week after the bonfire, I started secretly editing the manuscript again. I hadn't burned up my hard drive; no, I am not quite that fond of finality, or commitment for that matter. I'm a Libra, what can I say?

There's a good reason I kept it a secret. I didn't tell anyone I was working on the book again because without a doubt no one in my life would be happy about it. That's because they are not fond of the subject. They would prefer I just plain forget my first baby and his birth and death almost six years ago.

If not forget, they at least want me to tuck his memory into some flowery grief-closet to only be pulled out when his once-upon-an-existence is wise, or convenient.

Endlessly writing about the experience, they think, is not wise, or convenient. It is unhealthy, they believe. Trying to make the experience into a book, they think, is to not let go of the pain.

They can all suck it.

Although they may also be right.

I finally told my sister I'd been secretly working on the book again.

"So, you burned it like the phoenix?" she asked, kindly, but sarcastically.

Yes. I burned it like the phoenix.

Stay tuned to find out if I finally get the lipstick on the wriggling pig or if the whole barnyard goes down in flames (again).

Writer's High

February 12, 2009

Yesterday I submitted three essays to magazines. Last week, I submitted another to a contest.

It's amazing how after all of this time the submitting part of the writer's equation still feels so great. Even though cognitively I know the odds are stacked against me and that the most likely result is dreaded rejection, submitting still gives me a tiny little high.

This stems from the pride of having put something together, polished it and wrangled it into submitting status, and from the satisfaction of having searched for magazines/websites/ anthologies that publish essays like the ones I write, read through their submission requirements and dutifully obeyed.

But the kicker is that at the point when I stick my words in the mailbox or hit the send key on an email, anything is possible.

I have prepared and I have entered the race; that alone is enough to make me feel alive. The results are delightfully unknown; success seems as likely as failure.

It is the thrill of this possibility that gives the high. What if? What if the *New York Times* published my essay? How outstanding would that feel?

Yes, I know there are 10,000 entries a week. It doesn't matter.

This very moment, before the days start to tick by with no response, before the finality of a rejection shows up in my inbox, winning is still possible.

That possibility is hope, and hope is the primary reason we keep doing anything at all.

Will There Be Rainbows Day After Day?

February 15, 2009

I recall my days of autonomy. I miss them.

The proper writer-mommy thing to say is how lucky I am to be able to write from home and be with my chickens almost all of the time, too. This is absolutely true. We can afford full-time day care. I don't want it. I chose this life-work balance.

But it's also true that I pine for the days when I could do what I wished, when I wished, without constant I NEED YOU RIGHT AT THIS VERY MOMENT NOW, MOMMY NOW from somebody I know and love.

The chickens, yes.

But worse is Captain Daddy.

"Do you know where Noodle's rainbow shoes are? Have you downloaded my photos yet? The accountant needs to know how much we spent on childcare last year—can you look it up? Are you really working in there or *just emailing*?"

I must acquiesce to the fact that the only time I am going to be left in peace to work as I see fit is when NO ONE is in my home.

This happens approximately once a week. The chickens go to day care two, half-days a week, but somehow at least one of those days seems to be the very same day Captain Daddy is rattling around the homestead, needing some wifely attention.

So be it. I will bloom during my ONE DAY.

It is space-compressed blooming.

High-intensity blooming.
Real-life blooming.
Watch me bloom, in slo-mo.
Sloooooo-mooooooo.

What Matters Anyway

February 17, 2009

Chicken Noodle: "Mommy, I love you like a jellybean. I love you big as Mars. I love you all the way to Bluto."

RiP

February 19, 2009

"Blogs are dead."

This statement of doom was uttered by one of my writing-group cohorts at a recent meeting, roughly two seconds after I announced I had started one.

Naturally, blogs are dead. This is the story of my life—the thing I finally catch on to has already been dismissed by the cool kids. By the time I've hyper-analyzed some new craze enough to decide that the novelty/challenge/fear of it won't kill me, that novelty is cold in the ground.

There is a reason I named this blog Blooming Eventually.

Ah, well. So, I will be the one to persist with dead trends.

They can put this on my gravestone: "The fact that she'd missed the bus never stopped her from running determinedly after it."

Happy New You Part Two

February 24, 2009

In the course of one weekend, Chicken Noodle turned four and Chicken Little turned two.

After coming down from the sugar high, wiping up the hot-pink frosting and recycling the wrapping paper, I realized I have somehow become the elated mother of two gorgeous girls who drink milk from cups, walk on their own and sleep through the night. Not coincidentally, I simultaneously feel my life expanding once more to truly include writing.

My only regret is that I never really learned to trust the temporariness of the trapped-under-a-baby stage. If I had worked frantically through fewer naptimes would it really have mattered? If I had chosen serenity over obligation more often, would it have really made any difference in my writing career?

Perhaps: perhaps not. There is something to keeping the wheels greased, and something to honoring your utter exhaustion by immersing your mind in nothing more challenging than reading a celebrity profile in *Vanity Fair*.

In any case, it's not too late for a lesson to be learned. In nineteen months, Chicken Noodle will start kindergarten. Until then, I will fight to tend to my writing and mothering lives with equal parts passion and patience.

Things I Learned This Week

February 29, 2009

When, against better judgment, you let the four-year-old go to bed with lollipop, vowing to pry it from her hand as soon as she falls asleep, you will invariably forget, and instead find yourself doing surgery with hair scissors at 4:00 a.m.

Onward, Intrepid Writer

March 1, 2009

Six months ago, I sat down and banged out an essay about my grandmother. It came easily in an hour or two, the fluid culmination of thoughts I'd had since her death nine years ago. *Horizon Air* picked it up and ran it in their January issue. I could not have predicted the response.

Total strangers have tracked me down on Google and emailed me. My writing has been called "exquisite" and "simply beautiful."

One admirer said he used a line from my essay as his personal quote of the day.

A young woman revealed that she'd found, in my words, guidance for her struggles and dreams following the death of her father.

My favorite comment was from a self-professed "macho guy" who recalled his experience while reading the essay on the airplane: "I'm sure the lady sitting next to me was wondering, 'What is this six-foot-four guy doing with tears running down his cheeks?'"

This sort of response has only happened to me once before, with an essay I wrote about my father's experience in the Vietnam War. In neither instance did I premeditatedly intend to write a surefire ticket to readers' hearts. In a way, I suppose, that's what I always do, but what I mean is that with these two pieces at no particular point did I think, oh yeah, *this* will get them.

I am trying to allow this experience to remind me that writing is a mysterious vessel, and reading a personal practice. As a writer, you never really know what will make the macho guy cry or give the young woman insight into her own soul.

The fact that you don't know this is precisely why you should simply keep putting words out there; honestly, experimentally, sincerely, fearlessly.

Someday My Prince Will Come (and He Will Be a Literary Agent)

March 2, 2009

I haven't actually worked on my book in months. I rewrote the proposal last September for a consult with an editor. That's the closest I've come to delving in since those knee-jerk edits right after the bonfire.

I've needed that time; to digest, to recover. After all, the whole point of setting fire to the thing was to reclaim my life.

But there is also a problem, the same problem that's been there all along: I haven't figured out what the story is, exactly. That's the tricky thing about writing about real life; in real life there are stories within stories within stories, and separating compelling drama from extraneous details to create a plot arc is a wee bit of a challenge. Also, attempting this particular task can make you crazy as a loon.

The ending is a particular problem. It's got to be uplifting, because that's what sells, but since the whole book is about tragedy and death and monstrously massive grieving, it's got to be real, too.

Traditional happy endings—the kind with yards of taffeta and a soaring score—are for the plastic princesses scattered all over Chicken Noodle's bedroom floor. The rest of us have to claim the meaningful bits from every day and fashion them into our own fiercely-guarded raison d'être.

That's the ending I want. And I have to figure it out. I feel I should know this before I begin again (she says sarcastically).

None of which is to say that I haven't been writing. I'm always writing something. Mostly, there's my bread-and-butter writing, travel and lifestyle stuff for Pacific Northwest magazines and newspapers. Sometimes essays about my life. Sometimes tidbits about those wacky chickens.

So, listen up, Ray Bradbury and Malcolm Gladwell—I'm still working on my words and my hours! No slouch, here, nope! I'll get there, somehow, someway.

Free the French Fries!

March 9, 2009

During the last of three layovers Chicken Noodle and I endured on our journey home from Hawaii, I ordered us dinner in an airport brewpub. When the meals arrived, I reached over and snatched a French fry off of Noodle's plate and stuck it in my mouth.

Little did I know this simple act would send my overtired child directly to Crazyland.

"I want my French fry!" she wailed. "I want my French fry back!"

Never mind that she had roughly thirty-five similar French fries on her plate. She wanted *that* one: the one that got away, the one lost for eternity, the one elevated to idolatry and lament from today into forever just because it had disappeared into someone else's mouth.

It took twenty minutes of cajoling and a bit of fakery to convince her to get over it.

What makes us hold on to things long past their service to us? Why do we obsess about unfinished business? Observing this nuclear meltdown in my child, I wondered: what is my French fry?

Of course, I knew the answer before I finished asking myself the question.

It is my unpublished book and the hope that someone might publish it, which I have clung to like a rapidly deflating life raft, though if only I turned to look, I might spot a perfectly superior motorboat approaching.

I'm Not the Only One Working to Let Things Go

March 10, 2009

Chicken Noodle: "Remember that fish we had? It DIED DIED DIED DIED DIED."

Guts

March 16, 2009

Simply mentioning my book for the first time in months set off an internal maelstrom capped by a complete panic attack in the grips of which I considered quitting writing and getting a job at the mall.

This reaction would be amusing if it weren't so predictable. Since the first, seamless, innocent draft, pounded out on my keyboard in the two months following my baby's death, the thought of editing my manuscript has sent me into spinning anxiety.

I can never decide, no matter how much I prod my mind and my soul, if this anxiety is a normal reaction to a monumental task like writing a book or a sign I shouldn't be writing this particular book.

I recently read in *The New Yorker* that David Foster Wallace said, "The big distinction between good art and so-so art lies in being willing to sort of die in order to move the reader."

I don't purport to be nearly as intellectual as Foster Wallace, and he wrote fiction, but I will be brave enough to suggest this statement might be even truer when one is writing memoir.

When I think about what I will have to scrutinize, parse out and reveal about myself to make this book truly good, I kind of want to throw up.

It's exciting to think this could be possible and moving to an audience, and terrifying to think about how difficult it will be and how, should I fail, I will have simply laid my guts out on the table to be picked apart by vultures. Ripped my heart out and thrown it on the flaming barbecue. Revealed my deepest secrets only to be strung up in the public square.

These are not pretty metaphors, people.

And look what became of David Foster Wallace, anyway.

Chicken Noodle Speaks the (Unwelcome) Truth

March 19, 2009

"Jiggle jiggle! Mommy, know why your bee-hind jiggles? Because you're old!"

Chicken Noodle made this declaration two days ago after sneaking up on me in my closet while I was getting dressed. I couldn't help it; I laughed like Homer Simpson. Ha HA!

Perhaps the sensible reaction would be to tear at my hair in lament. But I have roughly eighteen months and twenty-one days to enjoy until I hit forty, and until then all accusations of agedness will be met with hysterical laughter (even if the emphasis is on hysterical).

Just for the record, no comments on the gelatinousness of my behind will be allowed by those over the age of five, now or eighteen months from now. In case any of you were so inclined (Ahem, Captain Daddy).

Addicted to Love

March 23, 2009

At last summer's Willamette Writers Conference, I won the silent auction on a consult with a publishing pro. I've been sitting on it for seven months, seized up in indecision and doubt (what's new), but felt I needed to use the darn thing, so I scheduled a meeting to examine my query letter in a couple of weeks. That finally pushed me over the edge into editing the manuscript again.

Strange things happen once I dive into that story once more. Excuses slip away. *Not enough time?* I steal time. From chores, from writing assignments, from my chickens. Even from cocktail hour.

Not enough motivation? There's too much. I can't focus on anything else. I work on my book all of the time. When I am not working on it, I think about it.

Too many interruptions? Well, yeah. That's life.

All of my other writing work starts to look like a cake walk. I whip out 1000-word articles in an hour. I edit in my sleep.

I become consumed. Utterly entrenched. A tiny bit addicted. And it feels sooo good. I feel like a bird, flying into possibility, soaring into the sky, heart a-flutter.

Here is why I hovered outside of my manuscript for so long. Diving in means submerging. And submerging is not something I really have the luxury for in my current life status.

It takes incredible focus to keep 225 pages in my head. One side effect is that everything else starts to feel like a frustrating distraction: Captain Daddy, my paid writing assignments, the laundry, my taxes and yes, those beautiful babies of mine.

One of the reasons I burned up my book was that it was taking me away from my chickens. Here I am once more. I don't want anything right now but this feeling, just the sense of flying in the atmosphere of the book.

Every time I am pulled away from the manuscript (which is often) I am subject to creeping anxiety—fear that the whole thing will crumble into a million little pieces without my constant vigil.

It's a great Zen exercise, actually: working on staying present with the book and staying present with that which interrupts it. And, as always, not giving in to fear, my constant companion.

But I can't help but wonder where all of this will lead. Editing this book feels so good now, but I remember how really bad it all felt eventually, the last time I dove into this little project.

Like they say, falling can feel like flying for a little while.

But Back to What Matters

March 31, 2009

Chicken Little: "Mom, I love you. I love you to the lamp, and then to space, and then back to the floor. But I love sissy to space, then to the lamp, then to the crib. So, I love her more, you know."

Look What I Made Today!

April 9, 2009

Chicken Noodle keeps catching me putting her drawings in the recycling bin.

She never once considers that I've done it on purpose. She always assumes it's been a mistake.

"Mommy, you accidentally put *this* in *there*," she says, holding it out to me.

"Whoops!" I reply and plop it back on the refrigerator with a big strong magnet.

This innocence, I covet desperately. Oh, to be so certain that everything you've created will be unconditionally cherished.

On my hard drive are three distinct drafts of my book. The first two I offered to the world like Noodle offers her art, with faith that some of the love I'd put into it would come back my way like a long warm hug.

Both were loved by several someones. (Thank you. You know who you are.)

Each was rejected by more someones. (Dismissal by agents and editors is one thing; by those who call themselves your closest friends another much more painful thing—but that's a story for another time.)

Rejection and disappointment are just part of life as a grown-up.

The funny thing is, despite hard-won appreciation for the harshness of reality, I still have a glimmer of that innocent, hopeful kid in me. Without that kid, I probably wouldn't keep doing this. I sure as heck wouldn't be on draft four.

Maybe I'll just move Noodle's art from the fridge to a big gigantic pile in the hall closet, clearing out of the way clothes and old books and umbrellas, keeping and loving every single crayon masterpiece she makes forever.

It's the least I could do, really.

Oh, Easter, You Son of a Bitch

April 13, 2009

The pressures of parenthood seem to congeal around a holiday like grease on a ham.

We *should* put the chickens in their matching dresses. We *should* achieve a lovely family picture. We *should* dote on the kids (at least not park them in front of a video). We *shouldn't* let them eat too much sugar. The day *should* be extra special.

Take that heavy carton of adult expectations. Add two children under the age of five. Throw in three pounds of candy. Tack on an early morning ETA at the grandparent's house. Shake well.

By 8:00 a.m. I've bathed the chickens and begun to wrestle them into their Easter finery. Except that Chicken Noodle refuses to wear her green-with-pink-roses Easter dress. She insists on wearing her white-with-red-roses Christmas dress.

Whatever.

I get in the shower and practice deep breathing, trying to remember it's not about dresses.

I *should* have mentioned this to Captain Daddy, however. I find him in the kitchen towering over a wailing Chicken Little; clutched in his raised hand is a dripping cup of yogurt. "You're ruining your dress!" he hollers. "No more until pictures!"

Note to parents everywhere: if you find yourself denying your children breakfast in favor of a hunk of linen and lace, you might want to reexamine your priorities.

Fast-forward through much more yelling and prancing about. Eventually we all move in the general direction of the car. Chicken Little face-plants in a pile of dirt and gravel in the driveway. Instead of doing something gratuitous like comforting her, Captain Daddy throws up his arms. "I give up! This is impossible!"

"That's why I've decided not to care," I reply levelly.

He considers this. "Hmm, okay. Sounds good."

Two hours later, both chickens have torn into enormous Easter baskets. They've consumed approximately one and a half pounds of candy each.

Chicken Little's dress is covered in chocolate, markers, syrup, strawberries, apple juice and crayons.

Chicken Noodle's dress is crumpled in the corner; she is stark naked.

We've taken a mess of terrible photos.

Captain Daddy is slumped in a chair reading the newspaper. I am lying prone on the living room floor staring stupidly at the ceiling.

We spend the rest of the day napping and watching videos. Everyone is entirely happy. And you know? It feels pretty damn special.

Burniversary

April 17, 2009

"When you set fire to something, man, you've got to respect that." More on this tidbit of wisdom and who said it in a minute, after I wax philosophical on cruel twists of fate.

You know how sometimes you think you know what you want, and you hope that's what you're going to get, and instead you get something totally different, something that ahead of time you would have considered to be the most awful outcome, and yet when you get it you know without a doubt it was what you needed?

Yeah. That. I guess the Rolling Stones sang about that particular existential comeuppance, didn't they?

The anniversary of my book burning was Monday. I forgot all about it because I was totally focused on the consult to work on the book's query, which was Wednesday in Portland.

What did I want from this consult? I suppose I wanted my teacher to tell me my query had merit, my book had possibility, and the last five years of my life spent toiling on this manuscript haven't been a totally wasted and painful time-suck with no possible positive end.

Basically, she said that last thing. The wasted-time-suck thing. The five-years-toiling, not-going-to-end-well thing.

I needed to dive into my book again. I thought that was because I believed the project had potential. Now I think maybe it was because I needed to be reminded of why I set fire to the damn thing in the first place.

My consult pro said, "When you set fire to something, man, you've got to respect that."

Other helpful yet devastating words that came out of her mouth in one short, tragic hour:

"Memoir is the hardest genre to write."
"Memoir is best written years after the events it discusses."
"Memoir is currently dead weight in the marketplace."
"Writing shouldn't be this hard."
"The book's thesis is still unclear."
"There is no obvious audience for this book. The topic is too hard."
"You needed to write this for yourself and your son, not because it's a saleable memoir."
"You are an essayist. You should write essays."

Ouch. She didn't really hold back, did she?

But I know she's right. I really do.

Okay, so. Add to that the reasons I burned the thing last year, which have come rushing back to me like a backdraft (ha ha) since I picked the cursed thing up again.

Having allowed five days for this potentially identity-shattering conclusion to sink in, I feel quite at peace. Letting go (again) of a project I spent half a decade on? Sure, sounds great. Can we have cocktails, after? I'm particular to margaritas: rocks, not too sweet, salted rim.

It's possible I am delusional about the peace part. But I did an awful lot of crying on the drive home from Portland and I think this time, I'm just going to opt to keep the peace. It's mine. I have freaking earned every last ounce of it.

Not sure what I'll do next, besides essay. Maybe chick lit? Needlepoint? Teach the chickens to tightrope? Stay tuned.

Things I Learned This Week

April 22, 2009

Taking small, temporary mental vacations throughout the parenting day is fine, but becoming so spaced out that you hit your child in the head with the car door will only escalate your problems.

Play Nice Now

April 27, 2009

Yesterday at the park we ran into one of Chicken Little's daycare-mates and his mother. We got to talking about the preschool, how the kids liked it, which days they attend. Hers—Monday through Friday all day. Mine—Monday and Friday in the mornings.

"How does that work?" she asked.

I wasn't sure what she meant. I babbled about how some weeks it's hard to get all of my work done with only two daycare days, but she just looked at me and then gestured at the chickens and her own child, finally capitulating, "Well, they seem perfectly well adjusted."

Oh. What she'd actually been asking was if two daycare days were enough time in public to adequately socialize my children.

Ahh, the dangerous waters of early motherhood, where total strangers worry not whether their own eighteen-month-old is getting enough time with his mother but whether your children are turning into batty old hermits locked away at home all day.

I don't worry about that, by the way. If Chicken Little and Chicken Noodle turn into batty old hermits it will be family tradition more than conditioning and therefore, unavoidable.

I do worry those two daycare days a week will have serious impact on my dreams of publishing a book. Especially since I've just trashed five years of work, have no clue what sort of book I want to write next, and realize even more than ever how very much hard work and time it takes to get published.

And, there is a deadline on even this two-days-of-freedom plan. Captain Daddy and I have a deal. In five years, he retires, and I get a job.

But none of that matters, really. I could choose to super-turbo into a swirling tornado of fear about this, of course, but—the chickens' socialization be damned—I wouldn't have it any other way. I want those precious little demons at home with me.

So, two days is what I have. The only choice is what I do with them.

Yippee Ki Yi Yay

April 30, 2009

If writing were riding, I'd have fallen off the horse and landed in the ER more than once. I cling, stumble, trip and plummet to the ground, then get back up, like some sort of indomitable horse-loving fool (or masochistic zombie—you decide).

Here I am, back in the saddle. In an effort to get back on the trail, this week I have:

Submitted an essay to the *New York Times* Lives page.

Unearthed my children's book manuscript and beta-researched it by reading it to the chickens. (They love it. They giggle and ask for more. Too bad they aren't publishers.)

Brainstormed a Young Adult novel idea. Do I know how to write Young Adult novels? No, I do not. Do I even know how to write fiction? No, I do not. Does that matter right now? No, it does not.

Sunk my teeth back into the paid work I neglected during book edits (newspaper article writing, magazine travel article writing, magazine copyediting, exhibit copywriting—GO TEAM ME!).

Blogged. (Okay, I always blog. But it's got to count for something.)

So: enough with the life analysis and on with the living, already. I'll keep you posted, unless the *New York Times* calls, in which case I'll be doing cartwheels in the yard and drinking champagne, simultaneously.

Six Candles

May 6, 2009

Today is the sixth anniversary of the birth and death of my first child. There was a time when I thought it would get easier each year. So far, it hasn't.

First comes anxiety and exhaustion—a frantic stemming of the tide of pain. But it comes anyway—a massive tidal wave of grief. I cry for days. I mean, really, why not?

This year has the added-value of a new level of grief in the dead-baby department, as I now know quite well that will not be memorializing my baby in a best-selling memoir. That is not going to be what happens. I will not heal myself through creation of a beloved tome. I will not be able to justify my experience with the external validation of appreciative readers. Though I once hoped for these things with all of my might, that is not how this story will end. Carrying his memory on my own will have to be enough.

Every year on this day, we go to the cemetery. My chickens have been to their brother's grave every year of their life. But this is the year I wonder if Noodle might start to catch on about what this whole situation is really for. She has a little sister now; she knows "baby." She's experienced the leave-taking of her first goldfish; she knows "death." But I am sure she still has no ideas of the meaning of the word "cemetery."

I am determined to tell her the truth about anything she asks, without totally freaking her the feck out.

This morning, we selected objects to leave at the grave. Noodle chose a shell and a rock and announced, "I can't wait to go the party!"

"But we're not going to a party, sweetheart," I began tentatively. "We're going to the cemetery."

"Why?" she asked.

I dove in. "Before you were born, there was another baby, and today is his birthday. The cemetery is where he lives. Well, not lives exactly, but it's where he stays." I stopped short in this murky territory.

"But will we get cake?"

I smiled, confused—then realized: Birthday. She's got this much figured out—birthdays come with cake. "No, baby. It's not a party, it's just a saying hi. It's a thing we do as a family every year."

She seemed satisfied with this, so we all four piled in the car.

At the cemetery she grabbed a fistful of flowers, leapt from the car and said, "I am going to give these to what's-his-name. Where is he?"

I led her to the grave and read his name from the stone marker. She placed her mementos on the flat surface and stated matter-of-factly, "He's not here because he died."

Couldn't really argue with that. There isn't really much more to say. The book is burned, the baby is dead. The first one to reach total acceptance about the whole affair is the four-year old.

Noodle ran around looking at the other baby graves: at the flowers and bears and whirligigs that adorned them. She was happy and playful. Her delightfully oblivious little sister waddled around after her under a cool bright spring sky. Captain Daddy and I exchanged bittersweet smiles.

Who could have predicted it would be our own children who would be our best guides on this journey?

And I felt at peace once more, at least for today.

Too Old for the Party

May 7, 2009

"No one is going to publish a first novel by a forty-five-year-old."

This little curse was spoken recently by one of the members of my writing group. Today it reverberates around my skull. So many of my cohorts seem to feel our age like an ankle shackle, while still recognizing that in the grand scheme of things these are the glory days we will lament in another twenty years.

My writing group ranges in age from thirty-five to forty-one; none of us (obviously) has been on Oprah and each of us wonders if we ever will come close. Two of us don't seem to care. The other two pretend not to care but really do. One of those in the first category uttered the curse, perhaps as a way of shrugging off his own fear, perhaps as a way of taking the reins of his own destiny. Announce that failure is already yours and you are probably right.

Another member said that indeed her agent had asked her age when he took her on. "It matters," he reportedly said. "Publishers want to know how long their investment might pay off."

Is it true? I have been to a lot of writing conferences at which I've listened to a veritable litany of limiting factors and potential barriers when it comes to the publishing business, but never has anyone outright said, "Old people don't get book contracts."

And yet, we are nothing if not an ageist society. The biological clock ticks for much more than the ability to childbear. We love the young genius, the freshness and vitality of youth; we desperately fear its fading.

So thank goodness once more for Malcolm Gladwell's "Late Bloomers," for pointing out the mature geniuses in cultural history. To believe him, success *is* still possible for us decidedly past the summer of our youth.

At the end of the day—call me a foolish optimist—I still believe that good writing matters more than the age of the person producing it. And I think it's really freaking dumb to quit at thirty-eight, so I won't be, just in case you were wondering.

I'll need a bigger advance, though, to pay for the airbrushing on my book jacket photo.

My Buddy Malcolm, Always Here for Me

May 11, 2009

"We tell ourselves that skill is the precious resource and effort is the commodity. It's the other way around. Effort can trump ability because relentless effort is in fact something rarer than ability."

—Malcolm Gladwell, *The New Yorker*, "How David Beats Goliath"

How Many Words in Your Pocket?

May 14, 2009

Today at Blooming Eventually, we veer from the bright and friendly garden of words into the dark and scary woods of math. Our subject is Ray Bradbury's Writing Theory. Write three million words, he proclaims, and you achieve mastery of the craft.

What does that look like? Let's see if we can take a stab at how many words I have written.

Where to begin: Does school writing count? Let's say it doesn't. We'll start with writing I did just for me. So...a few essays in college at 1,500 words each, many more in the decade after college; that brings us to maybe 50,000.

Next: the nine years I've written professionally, during which there have been another many essays for myself and for publication as well as a several hundred magazine and newspaper articles. We'll say another 50,000 for essays and 400,000 for articles.

Do you think e-mail counts? Probably not: Even for freaks like me who are compelled to edit even the most innocuous email before sending. All of those angsty teenaged diaries? Who knows. Blogging? Probably counts, but I am new at it: we'll give me 10,000 words. Newsletters, annual reports, brochures, web copy, ugh, gag, blah, blah: 40,000.

But there is that book I wrote. And rewrote. And rewrote.

We'll give it a probably-underestimated 100,000 words.

That's it? (Locates calculator) My grand total life word count comes to 655,000 words. Wow. I can't even see three million on the horizon. It's like three states away. Maybe I should have counted the angsty teenaged diaries.

But that kind of puts things in perspective, doesn't it? I've been writing professionally for close to a decade and still am not even close to three million.

I'll admit I could have employed more focus than I have. Distractions have included but are not limited to: beach vacations, small screaming humans, vodka straight from the bottle, *The New Yorker* and cream cheese yearning to be scraped out of the DVD player.

(As I write this: "Mom! Boo Boo peed in her pajamas! Mom! A spider! Mom! Boo Boo broke my princess!)

Will I get there? I mean, the chickens will grow up eventually, won't they? Yes, you say, but vodka and *The New Yorker* will still be there, ageless and tempting me until the end. Whatever. I can drink, read and write at the same time. Just try and stop me.

Stay on the Damn Train

May 18, 2009

I noticed the other day that the job that I quit nine years ago in order to start writing is available. I was hit with this unexpected twinge. Would they hire me back, if I applied?

That I would even consider this is directly related to my current state of disillusionment with my writing life. The book is dead, I'm three states away from three million words, and being a writer isn't for the faint of heart.

I tire of constantly trolling for work, writing on speculation, submitting, inching along from project to publication, wondering where all of this is going, putting myself out there constantly in hopes of approval.

A friend pointed out that I shouldn't add "begging people to love me" to this list, as I did to her; that I should believe in my inherent lovability and put myself out there as a gift to others. She may be right, but when the demon strikes, he whisks away any confidence I may have ever had that I should be leaping out of a cake wrapped in a big pink bow to a room full of admirers.

Long before the book died, this particular ennui existed — in fact, it comes around regularly. And, no, I don't want my old job back. Asking for that is attempting to rewrite history — like wishing to be pregnant again, which I do occasionally in moments of temporary insanity. This time, I dream, I wouldn't vomit my guts out for six straight months. This time, my fetus wouldn't feel like a bowling ball the size of Texas wedged in my abdomen. This time, I wouldn't be a terrified, angry pain in the ass.

But I would. I would hate being pregnant. The same way I'd hate my old job back. This is the road I have taken. I am a writer. All fantasies aside of some other less crazy-making, more stable job with an easily definable future—like nursing, or accounting: this is what I chose, and this is what I am.

Probably I'd be the one totally batshit crazy, self-doubting accountant, anyway.

What it all comes down to (naturally—and hello again, my friend!) is fear. In this case, of failure. "OMG, I can't see the train tracks! I've got to jump off the train!"

But I'd just have to get on some other train, right? The trick is clinging confidently to the one you are on, believing the tracks are there even when you can't see them.

Things I Learned This Week

May 25, 2009

One of the nicest things about having kids is that, as a grownup, there just aren't that many people in your life who say to you, "Oooo, I like your panties!"

Like Lightning

June 4, 2009

When I was in my twenties, I used to say, "I write when an essay strikes me," or "I have to wait until it's all there, inside me, ready to come out."

What luxury. Possibility and time were abundant; pure, delicious creativity the only motivator.

If I'd continued waiting for an essay to strike me (what did I think they were, electrical storms?), I'd never have been hired back by any editor I've worked with in the last decade. In my experience, the muse does not usually choose to strike conveniently during naptime, when I have an hour to meet a deadline (if I am lucky).

My youthful muse has been trumped by responsibility and sleep deprivation. I'd like to find my new, grown-up, battered-but-better muse—the one who is more reliable, the one I can access more or less whenever I need her.

I know she's in here under my wrinkles and yogurt-smeared plaid flannel pajamas.

Baby, You're a Star

June 8, 2009

There I stood Friday night, hovering uncertainly in front of a microphone, way more nervous than I should have been, and gripping a copy of the *High Desert Journal*. I'd selected and rehearsed part of my recently published essay to read, waited and watched everyone mingle and sip wine, and now here it was—my fifteen minutes of fame.

I dove in. "We put on the Snake River just before Hells Canyon Dam on a steamy July afternoon."

Two sentences later: "Ba-boom!" No—not the sound of me, arriving. The sound of drums. Loud, exuberant drums from just down the hall. "Crash!" Oh yes; cymbals, too.

I read on, inserting sentences between a steady "Dum-ba-da-dum-ba-da-dum!"

Very quickly it became clear that a) the drums weren't going to stop, b) none of my eight to ten pretending-to-be-rapt audience members were going to do anything about it and c) considering these fresh circumstances, my reading selection was way too long.

I considered the (sensible and later wished for) idea of coming to a dead stop and instead opted for a "you-go-girl" determination.

The drumming got louder. "Boom-ba-ba-boom crash boom!"

I abandoned emphatic, meaningful interpretation, made drastic, haphazard edits mid-stream and raced through the dramatic climax of the personal narrative in which I almost drown.

Every now and then two or three drunken twenty-year-olds

in skimpy tank tops and three-foot heels—paying me no mind, as if I were a plant or a hat rack—would skitter in front of me, presumably in search of the drumming.

I sank into the absurdity, skidded through some lovely, deep thoughts about marriage and risk and fear, and closed to triumphant clapping from at least three people.

Two seconds after my flight from the stage, the drumming stopped. Of course it did.

But whatever—I simply basked in the relief that the whole affair was over and began desperately searching for a very large glass of wine to suck on.

When suddenly, a little fairy woman appeared by my side. "That was *wonderful!*" she gushed. I stared at her stupidly. "You are an amazing storyteller." Her blonde-grey hair flew in a halo around her head and her cheeks flushed pink with enthusiasm. "I *love* your work. I can't wait until your next essay!"

I mumbled a baffled thank you and, after a cocktail, called it a night. As I headed home, I conjured in my head my consolation prize—the mileage I would get out of retelling this story.

Now for the multiple-choice part of today's post. The moral of this story is:

As an artist, one occasionally needs to be reminded not to take oneself too seriously.

One gushing fan is enough to justify any artistic endeavor.

Humiliating readings rack up as much PR as smashing-success readings.

If you are trying to choose a creative outlet and find yourself equally drawn to writing and drumming, choose drumming.

All of the above.

Please submit your answer by 5:00 p.m. tomorrow. The winner will be awarded the slightly crumpled issue of the *Journal* read from at this very famous and noteworthy event.

Artist in Residence

June 15, 2009

Chicken Little is extraordinarily articulate for recently-turned-two, as well as uncommonly considerate, which means she asks permission in eloquent English before doing all of the fabulously experimental things that cross her gorgeous small person's mind.

Take for example these recent questions:
Can I throw my cheese down the stairs?
Can I walk on the wall?
Can I poop on your yoga mat?
Can I bounce my playdough like a ball?
Can I fly like a birdie?
Can I eat my eggies off my shoe?

The fact that she actually listens to my answers and generally abides by them makes me think she is the most magical creature on earth. I am biologically pre-programmed to think this, but it's a wonderful sensation nonetheless.

I believe two is the most unfairly maligned of the young years. Yes, there are tantrums. Yes, every time I turn around for two minutes she tries to launch herself off the furniture or liberate permanent markers from my pen jar. There are sleepless nights. There are power struggles.

But two is when wonder and affection explode. Two is when communication really begins. Two is when absolute, delighted distraction can still be produced from a handful of rocks.

Recently, Chicken Little absorbed herself in ad-lib experimentation with a tub of hand cream. While I was not looking, she discovered that her fingers laced with this particular lotion slid deliciously all over her face and into her hair, imitating hair gel to create delightful greasy spikes, a la David Bowie.

In this instance, she did not seek preauthorization, which likely bodes of things to come. By chance I discovered her admiring her handiwork in the bathroom mirror and wearing a very happy toothless grin.

I was laughing too hard to be mad. That's another wonderful thing about two—as the child is fascinated by rocks, the mother is fascinated that she has somehow created a child in possession of the innovation and ability to create a work of art with a few fistfuls of Eucerin.

My Name is Kim and I Am Writing a Novel

June 18, 2009

When it comes to new things, I put a toe in the water completely privately. Or maybe just a toenail. I try it out in secret; I don't talk about it. This caution is true about new writing projects as well as other pursuits, like guitar playing or pie baking.

By not calling attention to my endeavors, I seem to figure, if the whole thing explodes before takeoff no one will notice the massive detonating wreckage.

Oh, fear, *fear*—why must you stalk me so determinedly?

In an effort to be a little bit braver about my ambitions, I have an announcement to make. I AM WRITING A NOVEL.

I began brainstorming it a couple of months ago, outlined it a few weeks ago, and started writing last week.

Yep. It's true. I who have never written even a paragraph of fiction in my entire writing life, I who have always said I could not write fiction—I am doing so.

I am acutely aware of the fact that I have no freaking idea what I am doing, and yet, I am doing it. Whatever happens, y'all know I desperately needed a new project to attend to whilst percolating the ongoing debacle of my memoir failure.

My career explained: Throw things at the wall, see what sticks. Kind of like what Chicken Little occasionally does with her spaghetti. Will this be as messy? Most likely, but I've got some experience cleaning up after myself.

Just Spell Everything

June 24, 2009

Captain Daddy is professionally inclined to report on topics of disaster and death.

In our early years together, I named this litany of unfortunate events the Trauma Tour. Everywhere we went he had a story to tell: car into tree, drug-addled assault, slow and lonely decay, upside-down van.

Since the entrance of small precious minds in our home, I've tried to press upon Captain Daddy that perhaps chickens that are ages two and four do not need to be told ghastly and terrifying true tales on a daily basis.

Nevertheless, the Trauma Tour continues. An average morning around here kind of goes like this:

Captain Daddy suddenly exclaims: "A drowning!"

Chicken Little ambles over. "Where, Daddy?" He points to the newspaper, explaining a fall, a sweeping away, a permanent goodbye, as if this conversation with his two-year-old is perfectly normal.

I roll my eyes and gesture in exasperation. "If you must share," I say, "try to leave the chickens out of it. Just *spell* things."

The next day, he tries. "A p-i-t-b-u-l-l attacked and mauled a three-year-old over in the valley."

"Wrong words, Captain," I advise. "Try the verbs."

I guess if I'm throwing ideas at the wall, I should consider becoming a writer of death and destruction. I have a research assistant on hand, after all.

Turn Them into Very Young Accomplices

July 1, 2009

Overheard at the park: "Dude. The cops, man. Put the beer in the baby's stroller."

How's Your Self Control?

July 9, 2009

An experiment conducted in the 1960s by Stanford psychologist Walter Mischel tested children's ability to delay gratification. A child was left alone in a room with a plate of marshmallows, cookies and pretzels. She was told she could either eat one treat right away or wait until after the adult left the room for a few minutes. When he returned, she could eat two.

Most kids snagged one the minute he was out of sight.

The interesting part of the study is that Mischel followed the kids after the initial experiment and found that those who had been able to delay gratification became the more successful adults. The "high delayers" were willing and able to invest the time and patience it takes to, say, get a PhD.

I am infamous for my ability to delay gratification. If anyone would let me, I'd open my birthday presents the day *after* my birthday. I presume I was a high delaying child (Mom?). I graduated sixth in my high school class, magna cum laude from college.

But at a certain point, I started to question what I was delaying *for*. Sure, I had the fortitude to get through law school, but did I want to be a lawyer? (An emphatic no). What had good-girl weekends in college to become magna cum laude earned me? (A rep as boring as shit).

When I hit the job-hunting streets after graduation, I found all I'd gotten for years of struggle was the opportunity to rock the world with an $8.75/hour job working the night shift in a home for troubled girls.

That's the problem. Two marshmallows are only a great reward if you love marshmallows (I think they are yucky).

Instead of that crappy starter job or grad school, I started waitressing. Waitressing is all about instant gratification. Work five hours and receive a fistful of cold hard cash and a free beer. It's even fun. There are hot guys in the room every night and they'll buy you drinks and kiss you in the alley behind the restaurant. Who needs grad school?

But eventually my natural inclination kicked back in. Powerfully. Is there any career more dependent on delayed gratification than writing? After ten years in this business, I say I picked a doozy.

You spend months or years writing, wait a possible eternity for someone to publish you, and don't get paid until they do. One recently published essay of mine took eight years to get published. And we aren't going to talk about my book right now, okay? We just aren't.

Is it true, then, that the treat of publishing (maybe it's a pretzel) is still worth it for me?

I can see my name on a book jacket, and it looks far more fabulous than a law degree or 1,000 marshmallows.

Easy Street

July 15, 2009

I fear speaking too soon. Yet I'd like to report on my novel-writing project.

Just over three weeks. Over 13,500 words. Thirty-five pages. Five chapters. My dominant emotion? Bafflement. At how easy it feels.

I know enough by now to realize initial creation is always the fun and easy part of writing. And I know I am just beginning even that. Finishing will be work. Editing will no doubt suck, as editing always does. And selling it (should I get that far) will be Sisyphean.

But, nevertheless, I feel as if I am watching myself from a distance, thinking: wow, who knew she could do *that*? It doesn't even look hard.

Perhaps the root of my bafflement is that during the six years I spent writing my memoir it never occurred to me—never ever even once—that writing fiction might be easier than writing narrative non-fiction about my dead baby.

"Ahem," a friend responded. "Yes, I would think it would be quite a bit easier."

Who knows how this will all fall out in the end, but right now this is exactly the balm I needed to move forward as a human being and as a writer. Even if this is all it ever is, I'd like to offer up the teeniest yet most sincere thank you to the heavens for that.

It's My Party and I'll Cry if I Want To

July 20, 2009

Last night I said, "If anyone spills their milk, I am going to cry."

I was absolutely serious. Only moments before, in the frenzied aftermath of unloading two children, two bikes, two backpacks, a pink reusable grocery sack full of fresh-from-the-Earth produce, my purse, my work notebook, and a handful of smashed crackers from the car, and during the frenzied push to put all of this away plus create a healthy and sustaining meal for the chickens and possibly even myself in the space of ten minutes, I set a full, open beer down on top of a clothing hanger on the counter.

It upturned, dumping beer on the farm share produce, the work papers, Chicken Little, her tricycle and the floor.

What's that you ask? Did I open a beer the moment I entered the house? Hell, yes, I did.

What else is it you'd like to know? Yes, hangers on the kitchen counter are not unusual.

What was that last thing you wonder? Oh, yes, Chicken Little rides her tricycle in the kitchen quite often.

So. I wetted a few towels, wiped down the small wailing person who now smelled like a college bar, mopped at my notebook, threw the drippy farm produce in the sink, grated cheese, made quesadillas, rinsed snap peas, poured two small cups of milk, plunked it all on the table, and declared it dinner.

I sat. Then I said, "If anyone spills their milk, I am going to cry."

But when not two minutes later, Chicken Little did indeed spill her milk, I did not cry. I did not make a single noise. I rose, dampened more towels, blotted at the now-stripped-naked-as-a-coed-and-still-wailing small person, and removed all evidence of the unfortunate incident.

What's that? Yeah, you're right; I guess I should have known Chicken Little would spill her milk. She may be blowing the two-year-old set out of the water with her fourteen-word sentences and bicycle-riding skills, but she is still two.

I sat. Two minutes later, the phone rang. I said, "If that's Daddy, I am going to scream."

Because Captain Daddy has this funny way of calling from the fire station right during the thick of high-speed parenting hour. And then saying ever-so-helpful things like, "It just seems like things are so chaotic with you and the girls when I am at work."

But when it was indeed Captain Daddy on the phone, I did not scream. I informed him in my calm-and-competent-big-girl voice that we were quite busy eating a balanced and wholesome dinner, and that we loved him very, very much, and how was his day going, and no, everything was going swimmingly here, just fantastic, really, a nonstop breeze, in fact, and I'd call him—darling, my love, my rock and guiding light—later.

I threw the dishes in the sink next to the farm share and tossed everyone in the bath and read books and retrieved baba-sippys and Richard Parkers and sang people to sleep and closed bedroom doors and opened a fresh new beer and sank onto the floor and gave myself a big fat pat on the back for not crying or screaming.

What's that you say? Crying and screaming can be cathartic and restorative? Hmm, good to know. I'll try that next time.

Plot Twist

July 27, 2009

Well, a funny thing happened on the way to writing a novel. Let me set the scene for you.

I'm at a book event the other night. A speaker from out of town approaches me after the event. I've never heard of him. I learn he owns a small press that publishes books about Oregon. We chat.

Him: "What do you write?"

Me: "A little bit of everything, but lots of essays."

Him: "What are your essays about?"

Me: "My family, growing up in Oregon, stuff like that."

Him: "I've been looking for someone to write a book about growing up in Oregon for my press. Maybe it's you. Would you be interested?"

(My eyes bug out of my head and I nearly spit out my cheap book-event wine.)

Umm, HELLO. HELL YES to the YES.

Two days later, and I'm still wondering if this actually happened, or if the cheap wine was laced with LSD and I hallucinated the whole affair.

But no. It actually happened. THAT HAPPENED.

BOO YAH.

Is now when I drink champagne and do cartwheels in the yard? Nope. Got work to do.

Hang on, people, while I ponder my fascinating childhood, and whether I can write about it with grace and wit and insight.

And Now We Must Hyper-Analyze Fate and Happenstance

July 30, 2009

I have two major thoughts about this fascinating recent turn of affairs, from a meta perspective.

First, the universe has a funny way of handing over the goods as soon as the protagonist finally begins to work on letting go of her need to acquire them.

Second, words of wisdom from so many mentors over the years are absolutely true: keep writing. No matter if you can see where you are going, no matter if it looks as if you won't ever get there, keep writing.

Because: when ten years into your writing career you utterly out of the blue happen across a publisher, and he just happens to ask you a question you never dreamed in a bazillion years you'd hear, maybe something like, "Do you have a book-length collection of essays about growing up in Oregon?" you want to be darn freaking skippy sure you can answer, "Heck yes, I do. I have that right here in my pocket."

No guarantees on this one, I should note. I have a lot of work to do, and it must please. I am to send him essay samples for his review at my earliest convenience.

But no matter what, I must remember this moment as a big fat reminder that dreams should be stuck to, but never clung to.

No matter which way the winds blow, you will be fine; but never stop working for the thing that will make you leap around and dance like a crazy fool in your very own kitchen.

Novel, what novel? I shall be a bit distracted for a bit working on that which I've always loved: writing essays.

New Digs

August 3, 2009

For part of June and the entirety of July, during an enchanting little episode of remodeling our home, Chicken Little's bedroom and my office were one and the same.

This caused much confusion. I would tell Little it was time for bed and she would amble toward her "old" bedroom, only to find it gutted. She would look around with consternation and begin to cry when I wouldn't let her sleep on the naked floorboards.

I'd lead her gently to her "new" room, and she would point at my desk and computer and say, "Mommy's office?" Which of course it was, only now with her bed in it.

Other times, I would go to check my e-mail and discover a small person asleep on the floor in my office, crashed out on her ducky blanket with a sippy cup nearby as if she'd simply keeled over in place. I would pace and fret that the hard drive, left on, was sending cancer-causing electronic monsters into her gorgeous pudgy little person.

ZOOM—Fast forward through the remodel (really, no one should have to live through a remodel except the residents who shall benefit from said remodel)—ZOOM!

Voila! Chicken Little has a new room decorated appropriately with butterflies and bunnies instead of a fax machine and scanner, and I have (as Chicken Noodle says) "a fresh and fancy new office."

This was a move of necessity and functionality (now that Chicken Little is no baby no more, kids are relegated to one side of the house and grownups to the other) more than an upgrade for me, but I must say, I love my new digs more than I thought I would.

Now, if someone would just close the door...yeah...that's right...go love on Daddy, now...leave Mommy in her nice peaceful little world...Ahh...

Things I Learned This Week

August 10, 2009

When you realize for the first time that your husband has installed the doorknob on your new office the wrong way, giving the four-year-old the opportunity to twist the button from the outside and lock you in, the proper course of action is not to holler for help, but to lie down and take a nap.

The Ghosts of the Past

August 16, 2009

I am suddenly and utterly immersed in my own past. It began with the advent of Facebook last fall, which abruptly delivered to me everyone I've ever loved, despised, gotten hammered with, and/or made out in the backseat of a Buick with. Then came the request to write essays about my childhood, which sent me diving into old journals and quickly concluding with a violent shudder that perhaps the past is meant to stay firmly put.

But the piece de resistance was my twenty-year high school reunion.

Put 110 people with complicated pasts and pending mid-life crises in one room, add high expectations, a few cocktails, and the pressure to connect in a short amount of time and what happens?

Everyone loses their minds. Or at least I do.

I would love to report on these events, but since it seems not all of me actually made it there, it may be a bit difficult. I will try anyway.

Here's a smidgen of dialogue.

Overwhelmed blonde girl: "I have…memories."

Cute tall guy: "Me, too."

OBG: "The fourth grade."

CTG: "Yep."

OBG: "Such a crush."

CTG: "And English, senior year…there was…something."

OBG: "Oh, I am sure there was something."

That's pretty much how the weekend went. I had many semi-coherent, almost-meaningful exchanges with people who, I now realize, are a part of my ongoing existence only in my foggy memories.

I expected some sort of special bonding only possible between polliwogs from the same pond. I expected a fabulous party, an escape from my grown-up life, the chance to pretend to be eighteen again. Instead I got a three-day out-of-body experience, lots of hugs but minimal exchange of real information, a hangover and a bundle of sadness.

Why the sadness? Middle-aged angst. So many years passed, so many doors closed, so many opportunities missed, so many traumas and joys tucked away, so many permanent decisions made, so much living already lived. The last time we saw each other everything was possible. Now we had potbellies, piles of offspring and mortgages. Given the dazed expressions on half of the faces in the room, I don't think I was the only one suffering from this strange sensation.

I underestimated the impact of going back to my hometown and rooting around in my formerly-never-to-be-heard-from-again adolescence. Or maybe it's just that a weekend spent subsisting on vodka, double espressos and Safeway deli is a sure ticket to misplaced self.

In any case, it was surreal. The prom queen's husband kept bringing me drinks and telling me he loved me. A guy I've known since Kindergarten pointed at my face, repeating, "You were always so *nice* to me." I took the chickens to my favorite childhood beach and kept tripping on the fact that I was the mother, not the child. Some guy told me he spent high school mad at the guy who came between us in the alphabet. One of the few women who has remained a close friend told a classmate who couldn't remember my name that if he could, she and I would make out. (He couldn't.)

Oh, and there was a bomb scare. Someone tried to bomb the

grocery store next to my motel.

Perhaps it was one of us, we group of nearly-forties reeling from the realization that sometime in the recent past, the last breath of youth passed us by, and we didn't even have a chance to hug it goodbye.

Poverty with a Laptop

August 20, 2009

I returned on Monday to a kind-but-definitive email releasing me from the duties of one of my regular paid writing gigs. Nothing to do with my performance, etc., etc., it's just that they found someone cheaper and more geographically convenient to do the work.

This sort of thing used to completely freak me out. I'd spin off into anxious hyperbole, convinced that this writing thing was never going to work out and I should just give up now and get a job cleaning motel rooms or scooping ice cream.

As usual, anxious hyperbole was a waste of time. Something new would always pop up. That might happen this time. Or it might not. Ever since the first of the year, my clients have been evaporating. Thanks, economy of 2009.

But I refuse to slit my wrists over it. Okay, so my income is starting to resemble that of a sweatshop worker in the Philippines. I just put the chickens' gymnastic classes on my credit card. But what's money in the grand scheme of things (she says confidently, knowing full well that Captain Daddy will buy her toothpaste and vodka)?

My goal is to remain calm and see this shift of fortune as an opportunity. I need to get this manuscript to the publisher. Yes, it's speculative. Yes, I may never make a dime off of essays about my past. But by removing all other more remunerative projects from my path, the universe seems to be telling me to get after it already.

Stupid Mournful Thought for the Day

August 22, 2010

"No one can stop you from writing. They can only stop you from getting paid for it."

—Bobby Moresco, Hawaii Writer's Conference, 2009

Essayer: to try, to attempt (from the French)

August 25, 2009

I've been neck-deep into my work-in-progress essay collection. The challenges and joys of writing memoir have reliably reared their little heads, leaving me somewhat dumbstruck.

Narrative nonfiction is my very favorite genre, and yet there is no getting around the fact that it can be heart-wrenching, soul-searching, scratch-around-in-your-past-and-see-what-leaps-out, emotionally dangerous kind of work.

Writing essays has brought me great pleasure and deep frustration. Kind of like motherhood, but with rejection letters.

Here are a few things I've learned so far about writing narrative non-fiction/memoir/essay successfully:

You've got to be completely honest.

Completely honest does not mean you must reveal every last detail of your life (i.e., please don't humiliate yourself and/or bore people to tears).

Essay is all about voice. Find it, work it.

Don't think too much about the audience. Write what you write. If they like it, great. If they don't, they aren't your people and you must not worry about pleasing them.

Definitely don't think about the (potential) publisher, unless you are on assignment. You can't read their minds and trying to will only cramp your style.

Make 'em laugh or make 'em cry. If you can do both in one piece, all the better.

Concrete anecdotes, not general memories.

Trying to write something everyone will relate to is the kiss of death. Precision, not inclusion.

Essay is personal. Reveal yourself.

Even a powerful story needs literary quality to become a work of art.

Every essay must be about two things: something obvious and something deep and subtle.

Conclusions are necessary but must be understated. Never preach.

Search for the fun. If it isn't just a little bit fun to write, it probably won't be fun to read, either.

Do not expect to write anything truly fabulous when you are a) in charge of the children b) in charge of the gigantic child masquerading as your husband C) drunk.

Proceed without fear! (In essay and in life).

I have about 25,000 of the 45,000 words I need for an adequate draft. Stay tuned!

Bad Mommy

September 2, 2009

Last Wednesday, I sat with a cup of coffee in front of my computer at 6:30 a.m., trying to come-to after a sleepless night. I was wrangling edits to an essay for my book-in-process, already lost in thoughts of the narrative, the perfect turn of phrase. All else had faded away.

Suddenly Chicken Noodle burst in, arms aloft, and declared with delight, "Everything's *better*, Mommy!"

About what happened next, Noodle later recalled, "Mommy went"—palms to face, mouth open, sharp intake of breath—"Then she cried."

Because everything wasn't "better." Not unless you think two children who have cut their own hair to the scalp is "better."

Noodle's happiness crumbled in light of my tears. "Stop *crying*, Mommy! I'll *never* do it again!"

But after a half-hour, when I was still blubbering like a soggy idiot, Noodle went all eye-roll: "Mom, are you *ever* going to stop crying? Like, by *ten*?"

I couldn't stop. I wasn't crying out of vanity because their school photos were ruined, even though they were. I wasn't crying because they could have lost an eye, even though they could have. I wasn't crying because I left the scissors out, even though *gosh dammit, ya moron!*

I was crying because this little DIY haircut session was a direct shot to the heart, illuminating in full living color my primary, daily struggle: my work vs. my children.

Or put more succinctly: self vs. family.

My writing life lives in the same house as my family life. It's like having two lovers. The problem with two lovers is that one of them is usually neglected. I steal a few moments for Lover A and Lover B slashes her hair off in jealous agony.

When I finally got my sister on the phone an hour later (yep, still crying), she laughed. "Almost every kid does this." I continued to sob, insisting on my singular ineptitude and unparalleled selfishness.

"Seriously," she finally said. "*When* is this going to be funny?"

I sniffled. "Maybe next week?"

Here I am in next week, groping for the humor and self-forgiveness. As well as being practical. It is not possible for me to monitor every moment of my children's lives for the next eighteen years. We must sometimes be apart. I am banking this will build autonomy and confidence for all. Noodle and Little are growing up alongside my writing career. Both deserve my attention, and both may be better for the other in the long run.

Still, I am not an idiot. I hid the scissors.

By the way, the reason Noodle declared that everything was "better" after having removed her bangs? "Now I can see my forehead like you, Mom."

Let that be the final word on the subject: as long as my oldest daughter desires to emulate me, I must be doing something right.

Nine Lives

September 5, 2009

Nine years ago, I got married, turned thirty, quit my job and decided to take my writing seriously. I wanted to write professionally but had no idea how to do it. So I flew to Maui with my mother for the Maui Writer's Conference.

For four days I absorbed everything I could about magazine writing. I learned about writer's guidelines, queries, breaking in with front-of-book stories, features, essays. I learned about the *Writer's Market* and how to track down contacts and market research and how to pique an editor's interest. I took notes and avoided the pool and the mai tais (mostly) and learned so much I thought my head was going to explode.

I took it all home and worked like hell. Within a few months, I was writing for magazines. I know it would never have happened that quickly without that crash-course. I also think it wouldn't have happened earlier, when I wasn't hungry enough, or later, after I had kids and was embroiled in the full catastrophe of grown-up life with all of its complications.

Tomorrow I fly to Hawaii to attend the conference for a second time. (It's now the Hawaii Writer's Conference and held in Honolulu, because who can afford four days at a Maui resort on top of conference fees these days? Lucky me that my mother lives in Honolulu.)

It makes me feel retrospective to go back. Makes me think about that naïve, hopeful, determined girl. To just go for it like that—was that really me? And that it basically all worked out. Wow.

I've been to smaller conferences since. I've learned oceans more. Published lots, not published lots. Found out how hard this writing business really is. Gotten wiser. Made choices, made sacrifices, made compromises. Part of me thinks: I've heard it all, I know all there is, what more could I learn?

But there's always more to learn. I think part of why I need to go back to Hawaii is to figure out how much of that girl from nine years ago is still in me.

The Emphasis is (Still) on Eventually

September 12, 2009

"You hear what you need to hear, when you need it," said Kristin Hannah, *New York Times* bestselling author, at the Hawaii Writer's Conference last weekend.

So much wisdom and helpful advice was delivered at the conference. It was fabulous—better than I'd hoped. I absorbed as much information as I possibly could, but the message that kept hitting home—the message I needed to hear—was about patience.

Nine years at this game and I am losing patience. The threat of a "real job" looms. For now, I have two days a week to write if I'm lucky. I spent six years writing a book that will never be published. Rumors floated from the industry say if you don't publish a book by the time you're forty, you never will (apparently that little message of doom from my writer's group friend was accurate).

An interested publisher just brings new worries—if I don't give him something really soon he could forget about me or move on. Lately, I sit at my computer and feel pressured and restless. I am losing patience.

But in Hawaii so many wise people reminded me that good writing doesn't come in a hurry.

"Make haste slowly," said Patricia Wood, who published her first book to wide critical acclaim in her fifties.

Michael Arndt, screenwriter of *Little Miss Sunshine*, reminded me of the 10,000-hour rule of mastery described in Malcolm Gladwell's *Outliers*. It was true for him. Ten years of hard work until he made it.

"Your job is to enjoy the process as much as possible," said best-selling author Dan Millman, just to drive the point home that it is a PROCESS.

Of course, I knew all of this already, even if I sometimes wish it weren't true. My best essays have taken months—even years—to write. It takes time for the good stuff to bubble to the top. It takes thinking and breathing and playing and changing. It takes living.

I am grateful to have been reminded of this now, with a good project in the wings. I shouldn't expect myself to create anything of substance in a big fat hurry, nor to settle for anything that's not slow-cooked to perfection.

Sounds Great, I'm Going on a Cruise

September 17, 2009

Chicken Noodle to Chicken Little: "I am now the mommy and you are my baby and you have to call our mommy grandma."

Waah!

September 25, 2009

I read a discussion online recently about how, before signing a client, an agent will read his or her author blog. Naturally. For a writer, one major reason to blog is to create a body of work online for anyone to peruse, especially, should you be so lucky, a publishing professional interested in working with you.

Why do you think I do this, besides to fabulously entertain all y'all?

The point of the piece was that some agents say they won't take on clients who write about certain things, including how hard writing is.

Seriously with this shit! This is why I avoid reading online discussions. If I listened to everyone's advice, I'd lose my mind and never do anything because I'd be seized up in fear of doing the wrong thing.

Writing *is* hard. The life of a writer means facing tough odds, buckling down to lonely, self-directed work, being willing to ruthlessly tear apart your own words, and getting your self-esteem cremated regularly.

No, of course it's not as nearly as hard as many other paths in life, like being an indentured servant or dying of cancer. We get that, dude. I understand no agent would want to read a constant whine, but I can't believe all agents want to represent Pollyanna, either.

What is a story without a protagonist who faces challenge?

By the way, I'm almost done with the sample chapters for the publisher. And if this is an agent reading, let me just say for the record, it's just been a total piece of cake! I mean, like, writing is so easy, I just don't understand why everyone isn't doing this!

And, also, wouldn't I look lovely on a book jacket? I'll be the best author you've ever worked with, I promise. I am constantly positive and charming and have never complained once about anything in my entire life.

We're going to Potty Like It's 2009

October 5, 2009

Chicken Little is potty training.

This means I've been carrying pants and panties in size 2T in my purse everywhere I go, scanning new environments for bathrooms as a claustrophobe would scan for exits, and muttering "do you need to go potty?" in two minute intervals like a paranoid schizophrenic with bad childhood memories.

I have also been witnessed leaping in the air, giggling and shouting "hooray!" over a pile of poo and groping my child's crotch a bit more often than could possibly look right in public.

It's a funny time, potty training—thrilling and a biohazard all at once.

Little is doing great. Even so, twice I have dismantled the car seat—a gigantic hassle—once pulling it actually dripping from the car.

Eww.

After that episode, and before a three-hour drive during which I decided to take the bold Mommy step of giving Little, who refused a diaper, the benefit of the doubt, we three girls made up a little song.

To be delivered in a ghetto accent in a strong cadence, with some rhythmic finger pointing:

Don't go potty in your seat
In your seat
In your seat
Don't go potty in your seat
Bad idea

Fun to sing, educational, and another example of the new skills motherhood has forced upon me. I can now add "songwriter of potty rap" beneath "laundry expert" and "short-order cook" on my resume.

Meanwhile, Noodle, feeling the limelight shift to her sister, is reacting with predictable attention-getting behavior.

The other day she left a urine sample in a plastic cup on the front porch for Captain Daddy—trying to prove (I can only imagine) that while her little sister can now pee in the potty, she herself has honed her skills to accurate aim at smaller vessels.

Captain Daddy didn't rise to her bait. He stepped right over the cup and left it there. The neighbor discovered it later, inquiring of its origins when he came seeking my help with a bit of writing.

"Shall I test it for pregnancy?" he asked.

Dear God. A nod to stages to come (hopefully far, far, *far* in the future), and a reminder to enjoy the innocence of potty training, the simplicity of problems solved by simply dismantling a car seat.

Happy New You Part Three

October 9, 2009

My thirty-ninth birthday is in two days. Forty has been looming large this year: A Hindenburg blocking the sun inflated by the hot air of my twentieth high school reunion, Facebook, an offer of anti-aging products from my dermatologist and the realization that the odds I'll publish a book by the Big 4-0 are slim to none.

If forty is when the weight of the past is equally balanced with the weight of the future on a life-sized scale, all the taking stock and anxiety that comes with it might make sense. I see the two halves of life pulling at each other in a matched tug-of-war, the past desperately trying to justify itself and the future taunting with undivulged secrets.

I am a Libra; naturally I will provide a scale metaphor with overdramatized consequences.

I spent the last year feeling forty coming like a freight train, me the shrieking girl in red heels and fluttering skirt tied to the tracks. Count on me to get ahead of myself, fear the future when it's still ten miles away.

But now that here-comes-thirty-nine, I am secretly a little bit excited about forty, and not just because I have another year until it hits or because I've been promised a massively awesome '80s dance party.

As a wise friend said on her fortieth birthday last month, "My thirties were *weird.*"

Remember back in your twenties when you thought your

thirties would be when you'd get it all together, blossom into your whole, fabulous, confident self? And then instead your thirties turned out to be about forgetting yourself altogether in the midst of the new and utterly dominating identities of wife and mother?

Then there was the dead baby and all of that grief—holy crap, who could have seen that coming? And how when you had two minutes alone with your own head all you realized—with an existential thunderclap loud enough to summon the dead—was how totally screwed up you were?

Wait, who am I talking to? Sometimes I slip into second person when I really should be in first person because I want everyone to feel the same way I feel so I won't be so alone in the world and so I can pretend it's about someone else and I might be able to seize control of the situation and fix it.

This is because I have boundary issues. I just figured it out the other day. I plan to address it in my forties.

Things I Learned This Week

October 20, 2009

When, at the grocery store, you consider buying sleeping pills for your two-year-old who seems determined to rise at 4:00 a.m. every morning until the end of time, you must forgive yourself for your bad mommy thoughts, and when you do go ahead and buy Benadryl, vodka, children's Tylenol, melatonin, wine, teething tabs and cocktail mixers, you remind yourself gently the important thing to remember as a parent is simply who to drug, with what, and when.

Love vs. Fear

November 2, 2009

I've had a little note tacked to the cork board by my desk for a while now. A simple square, in my own sharpied handwriting, that reads: love vs. fear.

It's a reminder to myself of something I read not long ago. Everything can be boiled down to love vs. fear. *Everything*. How you feel, how you respond, the actions you take, the intentions you set. Break everything down far enough and it's love, or it's fear.

The concept was a little tough for me to wrap my head around at first. But it sunk in quickly and like lots of crazy enlightenment things started blowing my mind up in a hot hurry.

Let's say you're angry at your spouse because he spent too much money at Costco on a bunch of random shit you don't need. (No, of course that's not a specific example from my own life, why would you think so?) You're about to give him a verbal shakedown because you're so very angry. But what is that feeling in your pounding chest, actually? It's not anger. It's fear. Sure, there is anger, but at the root of the anger is fear. Fear of running out of money, fear of your husband becoming a hoarder, whatever the heck it is, it's fear, fear, fear.

Another response to the same situation might be that you catch that anger/fear before it catches you. You take a deep breath and think about how happy shopping makes your spouse, think about the fact that he's making most of the money anyway. And then you look at that smile on his face. That smile is about how genuinely happy and proud he is that he can provide for his family, even if the way he happens to demonstrate that pride is by bringing home a three-pound bag of M&Ms and so much laundry detergent that Chicken Little will be taking that very bottle to college. Seeing that and not losing my (err, your) mind is love. Perhaps some would call it complacency or indulgence, but it's love.

Or let's say you're crazy, crazy, crazy sad about someone that isn't in your life anymore. That's sorrow, or longing, or heartbreak, but that's really love. Fear would be choosing to never love again. Grieving that person is love.

In the school of fear vs. love, you start tearing through the layers of whatever emotions you're experiencing, and you get to fear or love pretty quickly. Grief is love. Control is fear. Letting go is love. Ego is fear. Compassion is love. Shame is fear. Risk is love. You might feel fear when you take a risk (I mean a risk with a potentially positive outcome. Not a risk like shooting heroin). But your risk is really love, because you are loving yourself enough to try. You are loving the universe enough to give it the chance to make your dreams come true.

I keep that love vs. fear note on my board not because I have all of this figured out but because I need to remind myself it every single day.

Chicken Little is going to need laundry detergent at college, anyway.

A Bloodcurdling Halloween Horror Story

November 11, 2009

Imagine a dark and blustery day, a room cast with shadows. A writer polishes her working manuscript. The publisher has asked to see what she has so far. She adds fancy words, formats, agonizes, calls on the universe for extra powerful positive thinking.

The wind blows like a demon outside her office windows. Will this be the realization of a ten-year dream? Or just another disappointment?

Zap—she hits the send button on Halloween night (well, not exactly. Three days later. But it makes for a better story this way).

Then she waits.

The publisher receives the manuscript and reads fifty pages within thirty-six hours. He emails the writer, responding with words so enthusiastic some are unfit for small ears. He loves it. "Really loves it." He "fell in love with the character, her growth and setbacks and little triumphs." Thinks maybe his press "can't do this book justice."

It is the email she's waited a decade to receive.

But she doesn't receive it. Unbeknownst to her, it languishes in her junk mail alongside a sales pitch for Discovery Toys. She doesn't want any Discovery Toys. She does desperately want her book to be published.

She waits, biting her nails, cursing every doctor who never

gave her Xanax. Even though she never asked, shouldn't they have just seen how badly she needed it?

Would the publisher have responded by now? Maybe not. Maybe she's a terrible writer. Maybe her essays suck ass. Maybe he hates her. Maybe the universe hates her. Maybe she should just end this insane dream of being an author right now.

She waits.

The publisher waits.

The email waits.

Finally, six days later, before she's had her first cup of coffee on a Tuesday morning, she opens her junk email box.

What is this? Could it be? Such amazing things said? About her work?

But the date—last Wednesday? Dear God, no! The horror, the horror! Do emails expire? Has he changed his mind? Has he decided she's ungrateful, crazy, drunk, delirious on Xanax?

She emails him back immediately.

She waits.

Shouldn't she be celebrating? Not yet. Not until the junk mail universe has righted itself again. Blasted junk mail universe!

She spins in anxiety. She neglects her children. She drinks just the tiniest bit of vodka.

Finally, the publisher emails her back. He wondered why she hadn't responded. He hasn't changed his mind. They have a lot to talk about. He'll see her next week.

Stay Tuned for A Terrifying Tale of Gut-Wrenching Distress: Getting What You've Always Wanted

Blooming Eventually, Repeatedly and Currently

November 18, 2009

The meeting with the publisher went very well. If all goes as discussed, my book will be on the shelves next fall.

What the actual heck? Next fall. Like, when I turn forty.

It's the strangest sensation.

Driving home, my brain was short circuiting. I have every reason to think this is actually happening, after so many years of it not happening. I am going to publish a book.

And yet…that moment is not quite here, not just yet. When does one actually bust out the champagne? When the book goes off to the printer? When it's released? At the launch party? When it's positively reviewed? Sells well? When the next book deal comes?

I said to my mother, "I just realized there will never be one final moment of victory. Just incremental triumph."

"Like life?" she said.

Which reminded me of a message a childhood friend sent me a few weeks ago responding to this blog.

The way I look at it is that women are ready to bloom at any moment. We are not the annual flower that blooms once in a lifetime, whose beauty is awed but is fleeting and temporary. We are perennials—ready to bloom over and over with the proper amount of care (love, sun, etc!). It is the person who thinks they have bloomed once and it is over who begins to molder. Sometimes we are dormant, but the bloom is always in there waiting for the proper care to bloom again.

Now is a perfectly appropriate time for the champagne.

Ahead lies more uncertainty and certainly more work, but it's too easy to skip the small triumphs while waiting for the big ones. I've done enough of that in the last nine years.

There is always something to celebrate, and I intend to start toasting. Care to join me?

Pie

November 25, 2009

Today, on the day before Thanksgiving, as I pull out my hair and gnash my teeth trying to get through some mind-scrunching edits on my book when I really should be in the kitchen baking two pies for tomorrow, I offer you only this modest gift.

"Maybe all one can do is hope to end up with the right regrets."
–Arthur Miller

The question is which will be the right regret? The unfinished essay or the unbaked pie?
I'll leave that to you to ponder.

Missing: Life Force. Please Return. Reward: Chestnuts Roasted on an Open Fire

December 7, 2009

Sing along with me: *And when you're up you're up. And when you're down you're down. And when you're only halfway up you're neither up nor down.*

The toasting mood of a few weeks ago has solidly worn off. Now I feel like this whole book thing is sucking the life force out of me.

I know, I know. It's what I've always wanted and I should be able to find the joy in it and by complaining I sound like a big fat whiner and nobody likes a whiner.

Captain Daddy and I got mired in a teeny, weeny Marital Moment about this the other night. Here's what I said, roughly, over a beer at the local pub:

The bottomless soul-searching necessary to unearth the history and truth that will make these essays good is like letting a hundred angry leeches feast on me from the inside out.

Sacrificing organic creation for "sit down and create something beautiful about Topic X—now GO!" is like the Bataan Death March for the fragile artistic soul.

When I sit down to write, it hurts. Metaphorically, but also physically. Like a tiny monster is taking bites out of my head.

Half of what I write is complete crap that ends up in the file I named "shitcanned" on my computer.

At the end of the day I want to slip into a coma and sleep for like seventeen million hours.

When the chickens run past me screaming naked with peanut butter smeared on their bodies and hurling sharp objects at one another all I can manage is to stare at them blankly as if they are a bad television show I would turn off if only I could muster the energy to locate the remote.

I am feeling, well, just a little bit done. As in DONE. But I can't be DONE, because I am not done. And there's something to be said for showing up and persevering, but sometimes maybe there is wisdom in knowing that one is just DONE.

At which point, Captain Daddy gave me a rather bored look that implied he's heard this all before, and perhaps I was overreacting just a tiny bit, as well as maybe whining in that particularly irritating "my pain is bigger than your pain will ever be" melodramatic self-pitying shortsighted totally Libra kind of way.

And he mentioned something about this being my long-lusted-after dream. And lots of things in life are hard work, especially things that are worthwhile.

Which made me pout.

But I know he's right. (Don't tell him, because he'll just do that "I was right" happy dance and I'll have to throw spitballs at him made of tinsel.)

Do you think I just need a break, and beautiful things will bubble back up to the surface? Or is my coma permanent?

Yesterday I took a rest by addressing 125 Christmas cards and holiday shopping for three hours in a fourteen-degree-Fahrenheit snowstorm, but the answer to this question did not become immediately apparent.

Hearts are Often Misleading

December 10, 2009

Chicken Noodle (Distraught, after a lengthy time out for kicking her sister in the head): "Mom, I know I need to listen to my heart, but my heart said beat Little up."

Bluto

December 13, 2009

Yesterday, Chicken Noodle got a flu shot. Afterward, I took both chickens out for ice cream. We sat together in a booth in a very quiet restaurant, relaxing for the first time in a frantic day.

After a moment my mind started to churn with all of the things I still needed to accomplish, one of which was to choose a gift for my book club members, as the one I planned had fallen through a couple of hours before.

"Hey, what should I get the aunties for Christmas?" I asked the chickens. I am perpetually surprised that they are suddenly at an age when I can put questions like these to them and actually get semi-useful answers.

Here were their suggestions:
A basketball
A Bend Brewing Co. tee-shirt
A turtle sticker
Snowflakes
A merry-go-round
An igloo

At this point, Chicken Little bumped Chicken Noodle's arm, ice cream spilled on Noodle's new dress and she punched Little in the arm.

I said, "Hey, don't hit your sister, or I will take away your ice cream."

Noodle pointed out that she'd already eaten it all.

This might have been the end of the matter, but Noodle wanted to go deeper. Where had her ice cream gone? Might I still be able to take it away?

After considering these questions, Noodle speculated, "You would have to knock my head off and suck the ice cream out of my blood."

These, I admitted, were not measures I was prepared to take.

Noodle said, "'Cuz you love me all the way to Bluto?"

I said, "'Cuz I love you all the way to Bluto."

Perhaps in lieu of an igloo or basketball, I could simply give the aunties ice cream and tell them I love them all the way to Bluto. It would be true, and I have a feeling they might prefer ice cream over a merry-go-round.

Could be wrong about that, though.

All Aboard the Attitude Express

December 17, 2009

Should you find yourself in an anxiety-ridden funk like the one *someone* (ahem) has been in as of late, take these specific steps to immediately remedy the situation:

Take a road trip. Two cars, three adults, five children aged five and under, 24 hours, 400 miles and many salty snack foods should suffice. Weather: freezing rain/snowstorm. Destination: North Pole, via the Polar Express.

The driver of Car #1 should get pulled over within the first sixty miles. Reason: swerving. After determining that a) she is not driving her minivan ass-over-teakettle drunk at 1:00 p.m. with four kids in the back, b) driver of Car #2 (pulled up on side of road behind this spectacle) does not have our back as homey drug dealer/arms carrier, and c) no children will remain sleeping on this journey, deputy sheriff lets Car #1 go and leaves the scene, never noticing the expired tags on Car #2.

Crawl into the minivan back-forty to deliver juice boxes, crackers, raisins and fruit leather to wee darlings approximately two dozen times. Hit head on drop-down video player every time. Start being referred to as the flight attendant, subject to cracks like "Passenger in seat 3B, your freshly roasted peanuts are on the way, as soon as the flight attendant is back from her gin-and-tonic break."

Delight in the appreciative sounds of Child #4, who

repeats from the backseat, "You're stupid, Mommy. You're stupid, Mommy."

Upon arrival in train station destination city, get lost and drive around for fifteen minutes.

At restaurant prior to train departure, Child #2 crashes head into table and splits it open (the head, not the table), bringing you *this close* to spending the evening in the ER instead of the North Pole as promised.

Ride train to North Pole! Children laugh and dance and play and scale the seats! Santa comes aboard and hands out hundreds of small, noisy bells! Grown-ups wish for vodka in their hot chocolate! Average people sing at the top of their lungs! Train ride never seems to end!

Send sister a text that reads: "Still on train. People are singing Christmas carols. Have been kidnapped and sent to North Hell."

Nevertheless: when you finally do get there, children's eyes grow wide and awestruck at the sight of the lights of North Pole, making you feel all mushy inside about your recently updated "Mother of the Year" status.

Upon arrival in overnight destination city, get lost and drive around for fifteen minutes.

Carry five blissfully sleeping children to bed. Purr over their adorableness. Stay up until midnight drinking wine and eating cheese and talking about life.

Get up at 5:00 a.m. and blink blearily into your coffee while witnessing five slightly less adorable children run laps and scream at the top of their lungs.

On way out of town, get lost and drive around for fifteen minutes.

At first potty stop, Child #1 steps in dog poop and then gallops all over every surface of car interior.

Come *this close* to running out of gas.

Respond to children's endless whining pleas to flight attendant for juice boxes and bunny crackers by making up a handy list of mommy whines. (*Wheedling tone*) "Where's my chardonnay? I want a spa treatment. I need some beignets *right now.*"

Laugh so hard you cry at least six times.

Soak up the utterly joyful insanity only children can bring to your life.

Arrive home punch-drunk and cross-eyed, but happy as shit.

Remember that what matters isn't choosing the perfect title for your book or squeezing just one more brilliant essay out of yourself before Tuesday. What matters is a) getting out in the world and doing the occasional completely cockamamie thing, b) good friends, c) oodles and oodles of love.

Just Another Bat Shit Crazy Writer

January 1, 2010

Well, I'm back.

You didn't notice I was missing? Just read some of that shit back in December, man. That was written by my evil twin. Between you and me, she needs to be institutionalized. Or at least heavily medicated.

In case you haven't gathered this by now, I am not one of those serene, surefooted writers who eases her way through creative days with persistence and grace. No, I am the kind who hurtles along like an over-stimulated toddler on a new Christmas tricycle, obsessive to the point of compulsive, until suddenly the wheels come off and I careen into the ditch.

At that point, deadly self-doubt and anxiety catch up to me in a swirl of black cloud. I frantically swipe about for my creative self, desperately afraid that if I can't find her instantly she'll never come back.

This fear builds. The harder I try, the more I can't write anything. I become paralyzed. I don't sleep. I don't eat. I just quiver there, in the ditch.

It ain't pretty.

It's been this way forever. You'd think I'd get it by now. During the years I spent writing my first book, I thought it was just the topic. Once I finished writing about my dead baby, this fear/OCD cycle would cease.

It has been remarkably easier to write about my childhood rather than my dead baby. But, guess what? It has been two years this May since I set my baby book on fire, and apparently, I am still the poster child for the bat-shit crazy writer.

At least I don't write with a pint of whisky in my desk drawer. Or a pistol. Yet.

Being as it is New Year's and all, I am going to make a resolution. Next time I get all bonkers, I am going to see it for what it is—indication that the well is temporarily dry, not that my career and identity are imploding in a spectacular, traumatizing, publicly-humiliating, soul-destroying end.

"Back away from the computer," I will tell myself. "That's it. Real slow. Put down the mouse. *Back away.*"

I've tried everything else, believe me. Nothing but time away from writing cures the frantic paralysis. I seem to require intermittent distance from a project in order to be able to see it again.

I can spend that time gripped in front of the computer, having a gigantic fear-cow and producing nothing.

Or go to the movies with the chickens, man. Go to the mall. No one cares if you're bat-shit crazy at the mall.

I am back in the saddle now and feeling perfectly excited and capable of finishing my book. I only have three essays to finish for a solid first draft. Of course, now I also have a newsletter and six magazine articles to write. Back in the early days of the month, I had no assignments—nothing but my book to write. But I couldn't produce a damn word.

No matter. As long as she sticks around, Madame OCD can do anything.

Happy Blogoversary to Me

January 2, 2010

Today is the one-year anniversary of this blog! Hooray! To celebrate, Chicken Little woke me up at 3:00 a.m. "I kattack you, big fat mommy!"

Me: "3:00 a.m. is for sleeping, baby. No kattacking."

Chicken Little: "Kattack kattack!" (Flying leap; lands on my body; *thump*)

Welcome to My Disaster Area

January 6, 2010

A couple of weeks ago we went to the house of a friend of Noodle's on a play date. It turned out to be the kind of house that makes me feel bad about my house. Not a brand-new shiny McMansion, no. Just a fixer-upper that's been fixer-upped.

You know, like what my house could look like, if I actually ever did anything to it. This house was sparkly remodeled but livable and personal. The children's rooms were nicely appointed, and their toys were arranged in little vignettes on shelves. Family photos hung on the wall in neat rows. Cupboards and wainscoting were painted fresh white. Furniture was perky, décor just so.

It was very lovely. I kind of wanted to move in.

The chickens and I returned to our own house, which seemed to have been mobbed by five-year-old Hells Angels in our absence. Mismatched toys littered the floor, piles of dishes mixed with art supplies decorated the kitchen, books were haphazardly crammed onto shelves, crayon covered the walls, stickers were stuck to the floor, the Christmas tree tipped at an odd angle.

In other words, it was exactly how I'd left it that morning.

I raced around trying to right a few of the most egregious wrongs, wondering how soon I could convince Captain Daddy to repaint the entire interior, before stopping dead in the living room with this realization.

I kind of like my house.

Even with Crayola walls and kid-art haphazardly taped everywhere, including the headboard of my bed. Even with a dozen slightly mutilated magic wands shoved in a vase instead of flowers in the dining room.

Sure, there are things I'd like to fix, like the unpainted sheetrock in the basement and the stained linoleum in the bathroom. But when I look at those things in better moods, I see not ugly imperfection but time—time spent elsewhere.

Time spent reading books to the chickens or hiking in the woods as a family or reading *The New Yorker* or writing a book or sleeping. Time spent in pursuits other than beautifying my home.

My chickens won't grow up in bedrooms with beautifully arranged shelves of perfect toys. They will grow up, for better or worse, with a clear sense of my values, which are: people first, play second, work that makes you feel good third, work that impresses the neighbors last.

This epiphany made me so cheery I put the pile of kid art back from where I'd scooped it and sat down with the new Sue Grafton novel while the chickens napped. *That* I won't regret on my deathbed.

Exactly, Darling

January 19, 2010

As a writer/mother, I point out author, illustrator and photographer bylines when I read books to the chickens.
A few days back while unloading groceries, Chicken Little pulled a box of Newman's popcorn from the pile.
"Look, Mom," she said, all wide-eyed, pointing to Pa and Nell. "These are the people who wrote the popcorn!"
I get so misty-eyed when I see my parental intentions taking root.

Average Morning Routine

January 29, 2010

It is Monday—daycare day. We've been up since 5:00 a.m.; it's now 7:25. Everyone is dressed and has been fed something in milk from a bowl; peanut butter sandwiches have been slathered together and stuffed in bags; I have even showered. Cool, I think. I can have the chickens there by 7:45 and be back home writing by 8:00. That gives me three hours before I have to finish up and go get them again. I have an essay brewing in my head.

But then, as we turn to the task of donning coats, Chicken Noodle notices that Snow White is missing. As the reality sinks in of this small plastic doll gone MIA, an entire potential alternative morning to the one I have in mind flashes before my eyes: it is not pretty.

"I have to have her!" Noodle screams dramatically.

"Can't we take Cinderella today?" I plead.

"No, Snow White! *Snow White!*"

We turn the house upside down, searching for the errant Snow, a frustrating and futile activity that nonetheless allows me enough empty mind space to begin obsessing about the writing minutes ticking away—TICK TICK TICK—and finally holler like a crazy person, "We're looking for two more minutes and then we're *going!*"

This pronouncement lights a fire under Chicken Noodle's anxiety issues (the root of which surely can be blamed on moi, given all of this crazy-person modeling, but that's another story) and she starts wailing.

Just then I hear a crunch-crunch-crunching noise and turn to see that Chicken Little has plucked a forgotten glass Christmas ornament from under the sofa and bit it in two, and now tiny broken bits of probably-lead-filled-glass are tumbling from her lips.

I swipe my finger through her mouth, mumbling, "Oh Jeez! Oh Jeez!"

"Ohcheese," she replies, spitting glass, while Noodle continues to wail like her hair is on fire.

In a moment of unexpected inspiration, I hurdle to the basement, retrieve Snow from the dollhouse, hand her to a delighted Chicken Noodle, and scurry everyone out the door into a rainstorm.

Now I notice I have forgotten to dress myself. I throw some things on that aren't pajamas adorned with sock monkeys, load the chickens into the car, and drive while they themselves remove half of the clothing I've just put on them.

It is now eight o'clock. At school, I redress small people, shove things in cubbies, give kisses, give more kisses, give one more hug, and depart.

Back at home, I am confronted by what appears to be the aftermath of a bombing. Cereal is mixed with broken glass is mixed with the remaining and tragically unloved princesses.

I clean. It is now 8:30. I have two and a half hours to write. The anxiety has worn off and has been replaced by exhaustion.

What essay was I going to write? I can't remember. I glance at the couch. It beckons. I collapse.

Well, not really. I am too Type-A to actually sleep my daycare hours away. But sometimes it seems as if it might actually be a more productive use of the time.

Net Zero

February 1, 2010

In a brief effort to make my homestead more palatable, I spent a half-hour scraping stickers off of my windows. Meanwhile, capitalizing on my distraction, the chickens took the colored chalk and made a mural down the hall.

One-Upping Mr. Nelson

February 4, 2010

Last week I was invited to a middle-school classroom to talk about being a writer. It was one of those moments that made me go "huh?" and look over my shoulder for the real grown-up/real writer who was surely standing behind me.

"Oh, you mean *me*?" said my inner ego, who is nerdy, shy and still only twelve herself. She violently fears a room full of eyes on her, not to mention she is certain she hasn't a single interesting thing to say.

But once I got there, perched on a red cane chair in front of twenty seventh- and eighth-graders, I surprised myself. I talked about writing and kind of couldn't shut up. I think my allotted time was ten minutes, and when I finally came to a sort of conclusion, thirty minutes had passed.

The students were totally engaged, asking questions. One kid even tape recorded me. I can only hope I was more entertaining and inspiring than the lawyer who'd launched this career series for them earlier in the week.

It reminded me that talking about what you love is easy. I love writing, and the writing life. I even told them—with pride—that when I was a kid I used to spend every recess in the library. Even though at the time it made me a complete outcast, I see now it was a crucial step in my developing identity. So there, Bangor Elementary.

But it wasn't about me, being there. It was about them. I told those kids they can be writers. All it takes is doing it, and doing it, and doing some more. Voila! You're a writer. I told them they didn't even need to wait— starting today, they could be a writer. One kid said, "So I could submit an essay to a magazine right now?" I said, "You go for it."

Which got me thinking about Mr. Nelson. He was my eleventh-grade English teacher. He was a curmudgeonly sort who delivered fill-in-the-blank tests with questions like "How thick was the rope in *The Old Man and the Sea*?"

Mr. Nelson barely spoke a word to me all year long. Then on the last day of school, offhand, without smiling or even looking me in the eye, he said, "You're the best writer in the junior class." I was so stunned I just stood there like the dead fish in *The Old Man and the Sea* (was there a dead fish in *The Old Man and the Sea*? I don't really remember. Surely at least one fish died in that tale).

I've thought about that moment a lot, especially given it took me another decade to decide to try to become a writer.

Mr. Nelson, why not mention that little tasty tidbit of teacherly opinion a tiny bit earlier in the year? Why not encourage me? Why not point me in a direction I totally wanted to go but hadn't determined yet? Why not be a mentor instead of just the giver of ridiculous tests?

That's what I wanted to do for those kids. What I wish someone would have done for me. Why not? There's always room for more writers.

Yin and Yang at the Pet Store

February 11, 2010

Recently I took the chickens to the pet store. I envisioned a fun activity with which to fill a foggy February morning. I imagined the chickens' delight at my suggestion of a goldfish to bring home—maybe two, if I were feeling particularly magnanimous.

What a good mother I am, I secretly self-congratulated.

Chicken Noodle had other ideas.

Once we got there:

"I want a kitty!"

"How about a fish?"

"No, a kitty!" She leapt around in front of the kitten cages.

"But look at these pretty fishies; aren't they wonderful?"

"I want a kitty, I want a kitty!"

I steeled myself for battle. Put on my calm reasonable voice. "Oh, baby, a kitty is a really big decision. I don't think we're going to choose a kitty right now."

"I want a big decision, I want a big decision! Please, Mommy, can I have a big decision?"

How many times have I asked for something small and cuddly like a kitten and instead found myself in possession of something clawed and unwieldy like a big decision? Asked for autonomy, got responsibility? Asked for romance, got marriage? Asked for maturity, got wrinkles? Asked for a published book, got the big fat job of writing and editing it?

Actually, the book writing is going quite well. It is prickly and unwieldy, that's for sure. Not to mention speculative.

But as once went a wise quote I heard somewhere—"The hard thing and the right thing are usually the same thing."

A decade ago, I asked for something small and cuddly—the right to live as an artist and forge my own path. I got something prickly and unwieldy—the right to live as an artist and forge my own path.

Isn't it beautiful?

But no, we did not get a kitten.

Number Two

February 17, 2010

When you are four, poop is hilarious.

Last night, Noodle and I corrected an overtired meltdown (hers, though could have easily been mine) by crawling into her bed and singing a few lullabies together. It was a lovely mother-and-child moment, the sort that seems more precious to me now that she's only days away from five, and mere months from Kindergarten.

But soon enough, the grand total of three lullabies I know became boring to my dearheart daughter. She wanted to sing something more upbeat. A tune with spirit. We shifted to this ditty, something I picked up roughly fourteen lifetimes ago.

When you wake up in the morning it's a quarter to four, your mind starts humming, you head for the door, you brush your teeth, ch ch ch ch ch ch ch ch ch.

But this was not fun enough. Right away, Noodle took this song right out of my hands and kicked it up a notch.

You wake up in the morning with a toilet on your head, your toothpaste is poop, there's pee in your eyes, you brush your teeth poop poop-poop-poop poop-poop-poop.

That was pretty good. She had a good hearty laugh at that one. But she could do better.

You wake up in the morning and go in the yard, it's snowing and there's ten people watching, you poop in the garden, it makes the flowers sick poop poop-poop-poop poop-poop-poop.

I cannot understate the hilarity that ensued. But she could

bring it even better than that.

You wake up in the morning with the King and the Queen of Poop. The prince of poop kisses you, you pee on the queen. You poop your pants poop poop-poop-poop poop-poop-poop.

I've always loved Noodle's giggle. It's like an old coffee percolator, bubbling and boiling up.

But wait. She wasn't quite done.

You wake up in the morning with the Wizard of Poop, the King and the Queen of Poop Oz turn your eyeballs into poop, your poop turns green poop poop-poop-poop poop-poop-poop.

"Noodle," I said, tears spilling down my cheeks. "You are killing me."

We both took a deep breath and gathered ourselves for a moment, exhausted by so much laughing. It was nearly time for me to untangle myself from her arms, turn out the light, kiss her forehead and let her fall asleep.

"Mom," she said after awhile, between giggles. "I have an idea. Now let's sing something silly."

It's Such a Drag to Have to Live in the Past

February 25, 2010

I dreamt I was pregnant with my ex-boyfriend's baby. This is impossible for many reasons, not the least of which is I haven't laid eyes on him since 1996. (Oh, and my ten years of marriage, though I guess that doesn't stop everybody from getting into this particular pickle.)

No matter—in the dream, this situation was very real and posed many problems in my current life. Did I shun the boyfriend, stay with Captain Daddy and hope he'd agree to raise my love child? Did I ditch my family and go live with this baby's father, to raise our illicit bundle of joy together? Maybe a baby was what we always needed. Maybe a baby would make him faithful, magically force him to appreciate me and love me as he never did all of those years ago. Maybe a baby would encourage us to put aside the self-destructive behavior toward which we'd been so prone.

In the dream, my boyfriend held me, spoke soothingly in my ear. He promised me everything. Of course, we would raise this baby together. Of course, there would be love, joy—all of my heart's desires and more.

I awoke with Captain Daddy on my left and Chicken Little on my right in the bed I've slept in for well over a decade—far from Portland and the past. Far from pregnant, for that matter (and thank Jesus).

I knew immediately the meaning behind the dream. The baby is my book. My ex-boyfriend makes a small but illustrious appearance in this coming of age story I am utterly immersed in writing—the chapter he dominates marks the arc of the narrative. It was the lowest, most dangerous and chilling time of my life.

I do feel, by writing about this tale, by publishing and releasing it into the world, I am giving birth to that wretched time again. I am bringing events long-ago put to rest back to life. It's unsettling, to say the least. Memoir is a bitch, man. Of course I chose the gnarly scary potentially self-loathing genre.

But as Chicken Little woke beside me in bed, threw an arm around me and kissed me a sloppy good morning, the answer to the dream's central question was clear. Of course I would stay here.

To write about the past, to unearth it, to put it on display is to bring it back from the dead. But I don't have to dwell there. I can pull those things out of my personal history and still keep my feet firmly planted in the life I crafted from the Phoenix's flames.

Still, for the better part of the morning, I couldn't shake the image of my ex holding me so tenderly, gazing fondly into my eyes. Everything was going to be okay, he seemed to say. This time, there would be a happy ending.

Things I Learned This Week

March 1, 2010

Listening to Lady Gaga with the kids is super fun until you drop the little one off at daycare and she belts out to her teacher: "Let's have some fun, this beat is sick. I want to take a ride on your disco stick."

Happy New You! Part Four

March 3, 2010

The chickens turned three and five last week. I am still not sure how we all got here, let alone in one piece. But I suppose every parent feels that way.

At the park over the weekend, a father, while pushing his twenty-month-old son in the swing, asked, "How old are your girls?"

I told him, and he said, "Oh, so you're on easy street now, huh?"

Easy street? Is that where I am? I do vaguely remember things being more difficult even just a year ago. But I wouldn't say parenthood has morphed into a day at the spa.

Yes, there is very little ambiguous, ear-piercing crying in my life anymore. I gave away my stroller two weeks ago. If you hand the chickens a hairbrush, they just might brush their own hair. And I can say with utter certainty that never again in this lifetime shall I wear breast pads.

But these days, when Chicken Noodle finds my actions disagreeable, she lets me know with a vehement and entirely unambiguous insult. "You stupid pooty booty head, Mommy!"

And when I haul her off to her room for a time-out, she brings to the battle new advantages—forty pounds of muscle and a strong left hook.

And this morning after I started the bread maker and left the room, Chicken Little climbed up on the counter, got into the cabinet, and added several new ingredients, including dishwater.

And if I leave them alone together for too long, the scene inevitably transforms into four-star girl-on-girl wrestling, complete with biting, scratching and occasional nudity.

I suspected that Park Dad didn't want to hear any of this.

I finally answered, "Things are pretty great, yeah. But they just change. Some pieces get easier, some get harder."

He looked at me like I was a three-headed alien bearing news of the world's imminent demise. Then he chose to treat me as an unfortunate anomaly. "I can't wait until he's four!" he proclaimed.

The one thing I hope I'm learning after five years of motherhood is to quit waiting for the perfect tomorrow and start living the imperfect today. There's always icing-on-the-cake somewhere, if you look for it.

(Hot tip: look in the bread maker).

Try Die

March 17, 2010

It has been said that all fear is fear of death.

I've managed to wrap my head around the fact that all negative emotions are fear. Envy is fear. Anger is fear. Anxiety is fear.

But I hadn't gotten my head around all fear being fear of death until I began living with a kid obsessed with death.

Two weeks ago: after a half-hour lost to the ephemeral delights of Screaming Flailing Crazyland on account of who-remembers-what transition, probably that it was time to go to gymnastics, I finally cornered Noodle, gave her a fierce hug, got down in her face, and said gently, "I know you have a hard time when things change when you aren't ready for them to change."

Her face crumpled. "I don't want to grow up! I don't want to die! I want to be five forever!"

Whoa, dude. And I thought I was existential.

Today, on the way to swimming lessons, apropos of nothing, she said, "Is everybody going to die, the whole world, everybody?"

I've learned to just cut to the chase.

"Yes," I said.

"But that's sad! I don't want to die."

"You aren't going to die for a long, long time."

"But, actually," she brightly reconsidered, "I want to *try* die, like, die for a minute and come alive again."

"Well, sweetie, it doesn't work that way."

"Why not? I want to. Then I would know what it would be like, you know, for later."

Before I could respond to this (who knows how) we arrived at our destination ("Land Ho!" hollered Chicken Little) and I was off the hook until next time.

This will surely come, if not before then, in May, when her brother's birth/death-day rolls around. Unsurprisingly, Noodle thinks his little cemetery plot is the most fascinating place on earth ("Is he really *in* there?").

She recently told her entire preschool class about the cemetery and her brother with an enthusiasm akin to if he were, say, a newly acquired guinea pig. "We go and visit him at the place where all people go to die. He lives there, but not really lives, because he's dead."

To Noodle, the whole dead-sibling thing is like, seriously cool.

It's given me a totally refreshing take on that particular situation, I must say.

Things I Learned This Week

March 30, 2010

I went to Kindergarten orientation but failed to realize I was supposed to take my future Kindergartner with me. No one tells you anything, apparently. You have to figure it all out yourself.

Bad at Laundry

April 7, 2010

Yesterday, I pulled clean laundry from the dryer. With it, I found the shredded remnants of a small inspirational card reading "Freedom." Apparently, I washed it into destruction before I could even enjoy its blissful sweetness.

Drat.

I dallied in quite the dramatic self-pitying episode there in my laundry room, mourning the freedom I'd have to live my entire life without (as well as my inability to master the art of laundry).

Then, truth smacked me in the head.

Duh, ya idiot. You don't need a small inspirational card in hand to stake claim on a little freedom, or any other longed-for life state, for that matter. These things are yours for the taking.

Don't you get it yet? Make them yours, for God's sake. You're almost forty. It's about time.

Yay?

April 10, 2010

Chapter 238...

...in which our heroine is nearly finished with final edits on her book. In between fits of terror, she is quite jubilant. Honestly, she is.

(Well, she's sure it's coming, anyway.)

Fate

April 15, 2010

On Monday, I walked to a meeting. The route was a stretch of Nye Beach in Newport, Oregon. The destination was a local pub. The person I was meeting was my publisher. On my back, I carried 160 pages of paper—my book manuscript, completed last week and fresh from the printer.

The sun shone brilliantly; there was barely a breeze. I was all alone. Two miles of packed sand, open Oregon air and exercise lay between our rented beach house and my fate.

Of course, fate doesn't work like that. There isn't really one defining moment that sets a course of everlasting glory in a regular life. Glory is persistently fickle. Every happy ending is interwoven with the beginning of another new challenge.

I thought about a lot of things on that thirty-minute walk. How much outside validation I need from my writing, and if I can learn to just enjoy its creation and appreciate the successes that appear. My family and what really matters. How rooting around in your past and trying to craft it into something salable is as dangerous and messy as my friend Jessica said it would be when I started this project. And, just what the heck might happen during the next two hours—or two months, or two years?

But when I quit thinking and looked up into the stunning sky, at the powerful surf, breathed the sea air, I knew how lucky I am. How incredibly metaphorical this walk was! My story about growing up on the Oregon Coast was literally on my back as I marched down the Oregon Coast to deliver it to someone who would decide its worth. Sort of like the pearly gates, but with kites and sandcastles.

Judgment is still to come. But on the walk back, after a great discussion, with a pint of Oregon ale in my belly and my backpack much lighter, when the beach glowed even more marvelously and I felt like skipping over the sand, when I located my chickens chasing seagulls and Captain Daddy helping, I simply chose to revel in the glory for however long it lasts.

I knew the true worth of that paper-bound journey, and almost didn't even care what anyone else thought of it at all.

Wanted: Grammy-Award Winning Babysitter

April 28, 2010

Last weekend Tom Petty turned up on the cover of *Parade Magazine*.

"Guess who this is?" I asked the chickens. Expectant grins. I threw them a hint. "He sings to us in our kitchen."

"Tom Petty!" yelled Chicken Noodle. We've spent many a pajama-d morning dancing to "Mary Jane's Last Dance." Noodle can identify a Petty song in about two measures. (Ah, the joys of indoctrinating our young in our own sweet obsessions).

Noodle greeted Tom's image appropriately. She began kissing the page, landing passionate smacks all over his grizzled fifty-nine-year-old face.

"Oh!" said Noodle, alighting on a brilliant idea. "I know! Someday can he come and be our babysitter?"

Just putting this out there, Tom. I pay $8/hour. For you, I'd go $10. I know you're busy, so you pick the night. We're flexible.

Seven Candles, Burning Bright

May 6, 2010

Today is seven years since the birth and death of my first child.

One of the most challenging aspects of the whole dead-baby thing (yes, there are many) has been the inherent loneliness that comes with being the bearer of something so miserable most people won't touch it with a ten-foot pole.

From the get-go, the edges and depths of this experience were something only a few of my contemporaries even tried to comprehend, let alone address. I can count on seven fingers those who have really gone there with me in seven years, and a majority of them are bound to me by blood, married to me, or I had to pay.

Perhaps the death of a baby is just one of those life-situations irrevocably fraught with peril. What wasn't said hurt, and too often, what was said hurt, too. I've always known everyone did what they were able. I've tried hard for grace for that which they couldn't do. But that didn't make my experience any less lonely.

One silver lining of this whole affair (yes, there are many) is my chickens. Not just their blessed existence, which is pure healing balm and everyday joy. But also, for their reaction to this day.

I always intended for our family history to be something that was out in the open for them—not overly dramatic, but truthful. Every year we go to the cemetery to visit the brother they never knew. And each year, I am surprised and delighted by the ways that Noodle and Little transform the experience for us all.

Last weekend, Chicken Noodle began the planning. "What will we bring to him? Ooo—*candy*," she moaned, like it was crack cocaine.

"How about a bouquet?" said Chicken Little, who at three prides herself on her growing vocabulary.

"Candy," sighed Noodle, still lost in an imaginary-sugar-induced fantasy.

"Candy," agreed Little with a reverent whisper.

"No, I know," said Noodle, who at five has to have the last word, even if it means trumping her own idea. "We'll bake him a cake. But we'll eat it! At his cemetery! And we'll leave him one piece right there by his name. And we'll put heart candles on it! And we'll sing"—she broke into a warbling tune—"'Happy birthday, lovey boy!'"

All I've even wanted since that tragic day seven years ago was for someone to validate my baby's existence, honor my pain, love me there, and make me laugh. I could never have guessed it would be my own children who would do this the very best of all.

Cake. Noodle tried to tell me this brilliant idea last year, didn't she? And I missed the memo completely. Sometimes we have to hear things more than once before we take the hint. Sometimes, the youngest among us are the very wisest. Sometimes healing comes from a direction you least expect.

Cake. Heart candles. Singing. These are the very best ideas. We will make it so today, and it will be a tradition for ever more.

Fairies from Nowhere, Fairies from Somewhere

May 10, 2010

Yesterday, we took a big long walk in the woods. There was dirt and discovery and rain and running and falling and exploring and laughing and bugs. There was no crying or fighting or complaining.

When we got home, Chicken Little put a fairy and a snake in a chariot. They were on their way to the ball. The fairy's name was Rainbow Butterfly and the snake's name was Lola Rose. They were best friends.

At the ball, everyone danced and smiled. After the ball, everyone went to bed happy. It was pure and total magic, for one amazing day.

And Then, Other Days

May 18, 2010

Chicken Little: "Mom, do you think nature is beautiful?"
Me: "Yes. I think nature is very beautiful."
Chicken Little: "Well, nature is not beautiful to me. Stupid trees."

It Ain't Over 'Til the Fat Lady Sings

May 24, 2010

The good news: The publisher liked my manuscript.

The bad news: I have more work to do.

Newsflash: This is apparently life.

He said this: I have an amazing writer's voice. My memory of anecdotes and insightful moments from my own youth is incredible. My stories are fresh, alive with the Oregon vibe, funny and even insightful.

He also said this: Sometimes I am too eager to draw a happy-ending heart around each essay's end. (Shocking. Still looking for that happy ending, am I not?)

And this: The plot arc of the book ends about a third of the manuscript before I thought it did. Which means I need to shit-can the last five essays I wrote and create five new ones to insert earlier in the story, or I no longer have a book-length work with a satisfying storyline.

So, tra la la, back to the drawing board. Never mind, I had nothing else to do.

She's a Dream

June 3, 2010

Chicken Little continues with her early rising tendencies, though thankfully she's moved beyond the 4:00 a.m. hour. These days, she typically appears at my bedside between 5:00 and 5:30 a.m. "Mommy!" she says exuberantly, as if she herself has already had several cups of coffee and can't understand my languor. "Is it wake-up time?"

I always have a hard time answering this question. Primarily, because I am in a coma.

But, also, because no, of course it isn't wake-up time, it's clearly and obviously still sleeping and dreaming-of-a-Hawaiian-beach time.

But on the other hand, yes, simply the arrival of this small person grinning and shaking her mop of crumpled white-blonde hair and boinging up and down like a cross between Jack Nicholson in *The Shining* and Tigger in *Winnie the Pooh* means that, by definition, it's wake-up time.

Usually I just grunt and haul her into bed next to me with hopes that she'll go back to sleep, or at least allow me to lie there like a drunken sailor for five more minutes.

This morning she curled up under my arm. "We picked our mommy and daddy at the store," she announced matter-of-factly. "We said: not that one, not that one, not that one. Yes, *you*. And, *you*." She punctuated these last two statements with tiny jabs at my chest.

"Ummm," I murmured. "We are so lucky."

"And you and daddy picked us at the store. You said: not that one, not that one, not that one. Oh yes, THAT one."

"Mmmm." I was starting to come to. "Boo boo," which is what we've called her since she was little-bitty, "why did you pick me?"

She put her cheek to my chest. "Because you have the softest, warmest skin in the whole world."

Where are My Almonds, Dammit

June 24, 2010

A couple of weeks ago while I was on duty at my occasional writing tutor gig at the community college, I became suddenly starving. I emptied my wallet of quarters and headed for the vending machine, wondering if I would find any sugar-free, protein-laden options.

Yay—Smokehouse almonds. $1.25. I plunked my five quarters in and watched the little metal corkscrew arm make its slow rotation...and then stop. My almonds dangled there, caught on their own packaging. Then, strangely, a nickel dropped into the coin return. I gazed at it in my palm for a moment. Was five cents the returnable deposit on my risk? And how had I not realized I was taking a risk in the first place?

Stubbornly, I went back to my bag and got more coins. I didn't really want to pay $2.50 for almonds, but if I don't eat, it's possible I'll suddenly begin to stab my students with their own writing utensils. In went another $1.25 in quarters. This time, the twisty arm rotated, making its low whir, and two bags of almonds dropped to the bin.

Out of curiosity, I pressed the "coin return" button, and received two dimes and a nickel.

I scooped up my loot and headed back to my post, unable to shake the feeling that the whole experience was metaphorical.

Sometimes the world withholds your almonds. You do what

you've been asked to do and get jack in return. Sometimes you get unexplained gifts you're not sure even you understand. Other times you get everything you've asked for and much more. And sometimes, you just get caught on your own packaging.

Vending machine as karma.

This week, the almonds are good and stuck. I don't want to edit my book anymore, but I must. I am waiting for the coins. I know they're coming, sooner or later.

Everybody Needs a Drill Sergeant Sometimes

July 5, 2010

Chicken Little: "I don't want to hike. Carry me."
Chicken Noodle: "You start hiking down the trail this instant or I'll put you in time out!"

Sometimes Things Just Don't Work Out

July 19, 2010

Captain Daddy is over it. This whole "I have more work to do on my manuscript" wasn't in his plan. He's not buying it. I was supposed to be done with this book by now. I'm meant to be at the finish line, dreams achieved, *check*. He supported me for a long time, but he has his own passion project in mind to pursue, and it would be really helpful to him if I completed mine or gave it up already and returned my attentions to housewifery and motherhood.

But I'm not done. I'm still in the thick of it, dammit. I'm so close. I've been up to my eyeballs in pregnancy and grief and breastfeeding and bleeding over the typewriter for a damn decade now trying to become an author while still being a decent mother and wife. I don't want to give it all up and set my dreams on fire to selflessly serve my family. I don't even think I could do that if you paid me a million trillion dollars. I am not the same person I was ten years ago. I need my own achievement, something no one can ever take away from me because it's mine.

Meanwhile, helping matters not at all—my publisher has totally vanished on me. Vamoosed. Disappeared. Left the planet. I've sent him several emails in the last month hoping to clarify the direction and edits he wishes to see, and have received deafening radio silence in return. It's not junk mail's fault this time—I've checked 127 times. Maybe he's just lost interest.

Maybe he doesn't think I can do it.

And, maybe I can't do it. Maybe Captain Daddy has a point. Maybe I leapt for the brass ring and failed. It's not like distracted obsessive writer girl is the best wife in the world, that's for sure. Or the best mother, for that matter. I mean, everyone's alive and fed things on a regular basis, but my house looks like it was marauded by Hells Angels and I can't remember the last time Captain Daddy and I sat down and talked to each other about normal, basic, fun subjects. Our conversations are all about parenting or life management and address topics on the take-action scale somewhere in between "hair on fire" and "catastrophic emergency."

Is this book going to be worth so much sacrifice? Is it even going to be worth anything at all?

A friend of mine had an agent interested in her mystery novel but told me she just couldn't tackle the requested edits and manage the rest of her life. I thought she was out of her mind to give up so easily, but perhaps hers is the sensible reaction. Put the ridiculous dream in a drawer and get on with a sane life already. You were overreaching anyway. You'll be happier if you just settle into wife and mother and quit wanting more.

So maybe it's over. Why should I be the one to get what I want from life, anyway? How many people really do? Most of us just slog away, settling for a way to make a living and hope for some baseline satisfaction. I'm not special. Maybe it would be a relief to give up. Maybe it wouldn't suck to stop trying to fix this book, go drink a beer in the sun, and then go get a job at the mall. I could sell neckties or eye cream. Anything but books.

But I know it will suck to give up. A friend of mine is prone to saying that life is about learning to live with disappointment. I always thought he was just depressing as shit, but maybe he's right. It's amazing how much work you can put into something and still fail. And then you have no choice but to learn to live the rest of your life carrying around that failure.

My Little Mistress of Doom

August 1, 2010

Chicken Noodle's obsession with death continues. Here are some of the latest utterances from my five-year-old Mistress of Doom.

On the couch, cuddling
Chicken Noodle: "Mom I don't want to grow up."
Me: "I know, baby. But you know what's the best part?"
CN: "I am going to get old and die?"
Me: "Umm, no, baby."
(The correct answer: you'll be my baby forever)

※

At the park
CN: "When people are alive, it's way more cozier to be outside than to be underground, like later when you're dead."

※

On the deck, eating dinner
CN: "What if a tree fell on our house right now?"
Captain Daddy: "It's not going to happen."
Me: "You are totally safe."
CN: "But what if it fell right here on my chair and then hit my dinner plate? What if it smashed my macaroni?"

At Grandpa's house
Grandpa, to Chicken Little: "You're getting so tall!"
Chicken Noodle: "I'm taller!"
Grandpa: "Yes, but you'll probably always be taller, until you're grown."
CN: "Yeah, but I'll die first."

In the backyard
CN to my mother: "What if a meteor hit our yard while we were outside playing?"
My mother shoots me an alarmed look.
Me: "What can I say? She's got a little Armageddon in her."

Plot Twist, Act Three

August 23, 2010

I was sitting at my computer yesterday morning when an email popped up.

I read it like seventy-eleventy times to make sure I wasn't hallucinating.

(When good things happen, why is my first thought that someone has slipped me LSD?)

The email was from an acquisitions editor named Kevin, at a publishing house back east. He wrote that he'd been searching for someone to write a travel guidebook about Oregon for one of the press's series.

He came across my bio on the Willamette Writer's website, Kevin said. Then he "followed me around the internet." He read essays and articles posted on my website and Travel Oregon's website and other magazines and the like. Kevin even read this very blog. He said, "It's really funny."

Funny! No one ever calls me funny. I heart you, Kevin.

Kevin thought I'd be the perfect author to the book. He'd said he'd love to talk on the phone about offering me a contract.

I sat there in front of the screen for a long, stunned, surreal moment. Then I forwarded the e-mail to Captain Daddy to make sure it was real, adding a few excitable expletives as introduction.

Captain responded instantly and wisely—"call him."

So, I did. And Kevin offered me a contract on the spot to write a book.

What the actual hell, Universe? I am starting to love you.

I ran the stats on this blog. There are about twelve of you reading my posts each week, and one of you is my mother. So now I have a good one-liner for the book tour. It doesn't matter if there are only twelve people reading your blog, if one of them is an acquisitions editor.

The best part? No chickens cut off their own hair, ate poison, dismantled the video player, or tore each other to shreds in girl-on-girl wrestling matches during this entire episode.

We are making such remarkable progress around here.

Last Week's Pop Quiz

August 24, 2010

Quiz:

1. If you take the waffle iron out of the cupboard on a Saturday morning, open it up and discover an old petrified waffle inside, is it misguided to immediately turn an accusatory eye to the only other adult capable of using the waffle iron?

2. Should an (almost) forty-year-old woman really be expected to fit sheets on the top bunk? ("Mom, I can't believe you came up here and didn't break it!"

3. If you're at the public pool and one of your children tries to drown the other one, isn't that really the lifeguard's problem?

4. If you open your purse and find a half-sucked, half-melted lollipop embedded in its interior, would it be wrong to just throw the whole handbag in the trash and buy a new one?

5. If you're looking for stress release after a hell of a week, is happy hour with a three-year-old and a five-year-old the answer?

Answers:

1. He'll just deny it.

2. Darn kids should clean their own rooms, already.

3. The mother is always responsible, haven't you figured that out yet?

4. Take the money out first.

5. Hell no—get a damn sitter.

On Your Mark, Get Set...

September 1, 2010

I signed the contract to write the book for Kevin. My deadline is November 15. Like, *this* November 15.

Not even kidding. Wish I was kidding. Nine weeks to write a whole entire book? I've had longer to write a magazine article.

But never mind about that. I've been writing professionally for ten years. I've been training for this. I've been asking the universe for this. This is my marathon. Surely, I can churn out 65,000 words in nine weeks. No problem. I got this.

But I might need a little help. Madame OCD? Please get your ass up here right now.

Because of the tight turnaround on the travel book, the memoir is on back burner for a moment. (My publisher turned up again. Apparently his dog died and he was too sad to do email for a while.) Not to be released this fall after all. It looks a whole lot like both will release at the same time—next spring.

Not by the time I'm forty, but damn close enough.

Far out.

Someone suggested that with two books coming out, I should change the name of my blog. Nah. Lots more blooming to do.

I might have to update my bio, though. That book fire is finally and truly starting to feel like it harbored the Phoenix instead of defeat.

Good Advice

September 4, 2010

Chicken Noodle: "Mom you should make a practice book, and then if you mess up you can start fresh on a new page."

They Let Chickens Go To School?

September 8, 2010

Actual dialogue between my husband and myself:

Me (troubled): "You know what I think it is? I think I am anxious about kindergarten."

Captain Daddy: "You are going to do fine in kindergarten, honey."

If anyone needs me this morning, I'll be that middle-aged blonde dripping tears in the parking lot of M. Elementary. I swear just yesterday Noodle was a little package of love with a dimple in her nose who screamed like a pterodactyl when she was angry and got me up eight times a night to breastfeed.

Mama's so proud. Her little pterodactyl's going off to public school. Sniff…

In other news, I have temporarily shoved Chicken Little into full-time daycare. I see no other way to write a book in nine weeks. I suspect she'll live, possibly even thrive, though I'll miss that little nature-hating, daybreak-rising blonde bundle of perpetual motion.

When You Suddenly Realize Your Annoying Sister Won't Always Be At Your Side

September 10, 2010

Chicken Noodle, after we drop Chicken Little off at daycare, driving away, car window down, hollering: "I love you I love you I love you I miss you I miss you I miss you!"

Role Reversal

September 30, 2010

After school, one day this week:
Chicken Noodle: Mom, you be me and I'll be you.
Me: Okay.
Chicken Noodle: What did you do today, sweetie?
Me: I went to kindergarten. It was so cool! I love it I love it I love it!
CN: Oh, that's nice, honey.
Me: What did you do today, Mom?
CN: I wrote a book.
Me: Oh yeah? What's it about?
CN: Courage and love.
Me: Wow. I really want to read that one.
CN: You have to learn to read first, honey.
Me: Oh.

Fecking Forty

October 12, 2010

For all the thematic tension I managed to milk from my looming fortieth birthday in the course of this blog, as it actually loomed large, I barely mentioned it.

(Can anyone say denial?)

Well, anyway, it was yesterday.

I don't really want to talk about it.

Alright, fine. I know; you're right. You all deserve at least one tasty tidbit about this long-obsessed-over event.

Here's what my fortieth looked like from the outside: A fabulous '80s dance party with all of my friends! Love and balloons and tater tots and gifts! A DJ and tequila shots!

Here's what no one saw: Me, drunk and sobbing in the corner booth of a bar at 1:00 a.m., seriously swirling the self-pity drain.

I mean, everything is completely fine. Seriously, I'm fine. I'm on track with the book. Noodle is rocking kindergarten. Little has quickly ascended to class president of daycare. Captain Daddy and I even snuck in a fabulous trip to New York City the week before my birthday.

But now I see quite clearly it was utter folly to think one amazing party could compensate for an entire decade of complicated living.

And I don't really know how I feel about anything because I've been racing around like a deranged monkey fueled by espresso and goldfish crackers since I signed the book contract.

Whatever. I'm forty now. Onward.

Anyway, sometimes you just need a good goddamn cry. Doing so in a dive bar wearing the second-most expensive dress you've ever purchased is all the better.

Also, my mom was diagnosed with cancer.

On my birthday.

Yeah, that really happened.

And, completely sucks ass.

More Good Advice

October 20, 2010

Chicken Noodle, after school yesterday, back at home: "Mom, you should keep your shoes on in case there's a fire drill."

Vocabulary

October 24, 2010

Chicken Little, three-going-on-four, has learned a new word. She's been working hard to insert it in as many sentences as possible.

Where is my ducky blanket, dammit?
Dammit, I hate oatmeal.
Dammit, I want to catch a butterfly!
I need to go to bed right now, dammit.

Meanwhile, Chicken Noodle, five-going-on-six, has begun writing her own songs. She coins lyrics and a tune in her head before requiring us, her family and built-in fan base, to sit raptly while she sings. She uses a red rake as a guitar. Occasionally, like so many rock stars before her, she performs half-naked.

Her lyrics, unsurprisingly, are dark. Except for when they are inspiring.

We love the sun/the sun/the sun
but not the ocean
because sometimes you bonk your head
and get ate-en by a shark.

Wouldn't it be great
if we had a cat cat cat
who didn't bite us
and make us bleed bleed bleed
when we picked him up?

And we know in our hearts we are helpful and kind
sometimes we just make mistakes!

We can find the secrets in our minds
we can find the secrets in the stars
we can do it
we can!

I don't know why anyone ever thinks they need amusement parks, or Wii, or heroin. Children are the world's best entertainment.

Here

November 2, 2010

When I was young, Halloween was my very favorite holiday. No big surprise for a kid who was always yearning to be anyone but herself. Even if it was a fantasy, this was my one chance a year to be wilder, freer, happier, better.

The last few weeks have been pretty darned real, as was this Halloween night. No rock and roll fantasies this year. Instead the surprise gift was that I felt exactly like myself. And I kind of even liked her.

This meant I wandered around after two gorgeous princesses, drinking a beer straight from the bottle in the middle of the street with no shame whatsoever, wearing a fresh pair of Rod Lavers, an oversized witch hat and some cherry Chapstick.

With me were some of my very favorite people in the whole world and a pig on a leash. Iron Man was there, too, masked and ready to protect us all. He ran with the frilly girls from house to house and only once asked the Spanish Dancer if maybe she would touch the giant spider first.

There was camaraderie and laughter and love. For at least one brief moment late in the dark and starry evening, the whole world sat in the palm of perfection.

Right about then, the Pumpkin Princess climbed on my back, tucked her cheek into the nape of my neck and said, "I love you, Mommy."Why would I want to be anyone else?

How to Totally Freak Out the Trader Joe's Checker

November 9, 2010

Checker: "You girls are so cute!"

Chicken Noodle and Chicken Little (preening): "Thanks!"

Checker: "Do you have any other brothers or sisters?"

CN: "We had a brother."

CL: "But he died."

CN: "Yeah, he's dead."

CL: "Really, really dead."

CN: "Super dead."

Checker: "Oh." (Begins to shove things very quickly into bags, avoiding eye contact.)

What's My Word Count Now, Huh, Punk?

November 16, 2010

Well, I did it. I wrote a book in nine weeks.

I knocked out a 250-page, 65,000-word book in sixty-odd days. Sent off to editor-land yesterday.

Actually, apparently, I got a little carried away, because I accidentally wrote 75,000 words. To borrow Chicken Little's new favorite word: *Dammit!* Would this not have been a fine opportunity to taste the strange fruit of underachievement?

Here's what I learned in the process:

Writing is easy.

Writing is the best job in the whole world.

Writing sucks ass.

Writing is a hateful, evil, miserable affliction. Why didn't I become a rocket scientist, or an anesthesiologist, or an exotic dancer? Why, why, why?!

Stress brings out my over-dramatic side.

Writing a book in nine weeks will kick your ass six ways from Sunday, but nothing on earth is harder than parenting, which is what I had been doing with the majority of my time prior to this project. Therefore, writing is easy.

Thinking—thinking is what is bad. Must stop thinking.

You might think that for you to pull off a feat this enormous, everything extraneous will have to get out of the way. But trust me—life will just keep on coming.

My God, does this truly have to be this hard?

I really like almond butter and honey sandwiches.

There is a dust bunny the size of Texas under my desk.

There are a lot of really, really bad websites out there.

There isn't much that can't be cured with a DVD of *Entourage*, coral-colored toenail polish and vodka.

(However) Drinking and writing is not a good idea. No wonder Hemingway shot himself.

This is a piece of cake! Hell, I could have done this in six weeks!

My kids rock. Instead of resenting that Mommy was irritable and totally out to lunch, they bragged about me on the playground.

Captain Daddy is a superhero. Of course, we already knew that. That's why he wears tight shirts and funny shoes with pockets for the toes.

It is totally possible to write a book in nine weeks, keep the children alive, turn forty, throw yourself a big-ass party, navigate your mother's cancer diagnosis, talk your husband down from a mid-life crisis, spend five days in New York City pretending you are a rock star, question the entire structure on which your adult life is based, and, for a finale, get locked out of your house by your three-year-old when you are naked in the hot tub.

But I don't necessarily recommend it.

Still—once you've run the gauntlet, wow, what a rush!

Now if you'll excuse me, I am going to go slip into a coma for several days. Or at least until the school bus comes.

Reality Bites

November 20, 2010

Chicken Little: "I want to be a princess."
Me: "Well you can't, honey, because I am not a queen. I'm a writer."

Hey, Kimo

November 23, 2010

Last week, I took seven days off of everything to help my mother through her first chemo treatment—or, as they say in Hawaii, her first date with "my friend Kimo."

It was my first experience as witness to chemo. I imagine chemo looks the same pretty much anywhere, but here are my notes on Hawaiian Kimo. It's all I've got to offer y'all this week, so take it or leave it, babies.

Should one travel to Hawaii for something un-fun, small talk on the plane becomes more awkward than usual. "Are you going home or on vacation?" asked the nice man next to me as he sipped on his Mai Tai. "Neither. Well, both. Well, neither," I replied. Then I had to tell him the truth, which, turns out, from the look on his face, wasn't really what he was after.

On the morning of Mom's first date with Kimo, long before dawn, I watched a girl cross the parking lot below the condo, climb a fence, pluck a plumeria blossom from a tree and tuck it behind her ear. As she stepped lightly away into the darkness, somehow I was filled with the most delicate beginnings of hope.

A bit later in the morning, the most stunning, multilayered, salmon-pink-scarlet sunrise appeared on the horizon. I attempted to interpret this sunset as hope, too, but the detailed lecture I was simultaneously receiving from my mother about why I must immediately schedule a colonoscopy dampened my enthusiasm.

While we waited in the mauve-colored waiting room at the hospital, we were treated to the local news. "Home devoured by lava on the Big Island," intoned the announcer. A rather ominous cloud descended on me. (Though I'll admit that lava, live, is rather pretty.)

The blood on the floor of the Kimo room didn't help, either.

The hospital food looked exotic—rice, a hamburger patty, a fried egg, gravy (plate lunch, ya), or sushi—but still managed, as does hospital food everywhere, to taste hideous.

The hospital staff ranged in race from Samoan to Filipino, hardly a haole (white person) in sight. Somehow, this diversity of faces brought the hope back again.

And speaking of hope, President Obama's favorite breakfast place from when he was a kid is now a boarded-up spot in a strip mall, I was told as we drove past. Poor guy.

When I held my mother's hand as she met Kimo, it felt small and warm, like a seashell on the beach that was not far away but that I nevertheless wouldn't set foot on once all week.

When I finished watching chemicals drip into my mother's veins for six hours, got her back to her place, and put her down for her nap, I collapsed by the pool under the most stunning plum-colored bougainvillea bush and a handful of palm trees wafting in the breeze. This, I realize, should have been pleasurable.

And yet it is true that taking care of one mother is easier than taking care of two small children and a husband.

When I called home, Chicken Noodle refused to talk to me. Chicken Little got on the phone only briefly, to say, "You are taking care of Grandma. I love you, now, *bye!*"

Love—Thank you, Little—*love*. Love is where the hope lives, and there is so very much of it, and that's why everything is going to be okay. (And Obama probably has a new favorite breakfast spot, anyhow.)

When I got home, I tried to make Kimo into a funny blog post. I find that if I really try I can make just about anything into a funny blog post, and it helps make hard stuff easier. But I failed. Because Kimo isn't funny. Kimo sucks. Even Kimo in Hawaii.

I Need A Wife

December 10, 2010

Some writers, when finding themselves in the throes of just a wee dose of success, might hire themselves an assistant.

Instead, I'd like to hire a wife.

Duties include:

Finding more outfits for Chicken Noodle, who has announced she will only wear red until May.

Composting the pumpkins that are still on the front porch.

Scraping art clay off the woodwork from last summer's sculpting project.

Christmas shopping.

Painting over the crayon on the wall.

Redecorating the Christmas tree that the chickens already decorated, undecorated and redecorated to their liking.

Vacuuming the oatmeal out of the heater vent in the kitchen.

Addressing 125 Christmas cards.

Shopping for a disco ball for New Year's Eve.

Going to couples' therapy with Captain Daddy.

Recycling pounds of kid art without any kids noticing.

Locating a costume for Chicken Little's ballet recital this weekend.

Writing a book. (Okay, fine. I'll do that one.)

Start date: Immediately.

Pay: I'll pour you a glass of wine.

Applicants: Apply at my front door. If you have a heartbeat and are not hammered, you're hired.

Christmas Dinner Conversation Topics to Consider

December 25, 2010

Chicken Little to Grandpa (sadly): "Our brother died."
Grandpa: "I heard."
Little: "He was born too late."
Grandpa (lovingly): "I know, I heard."

The Unparalleled Allure of an Imaginary Brother

January 4, 2011

Chicken Noodle: "Mom, we're playing princess castle, and Little won't be the prince and I want her to be the prince."

Me: "I'm sorry, baby. But she gets to be what she wants." Noodle: "If our brother were alive, he'd be the prince."

Me: "Yeah, maybe."

Noodle: "And there would be more of us to play when we play Crazy 8's."

Me: "Yes."

Noodle: "It's not fair."

Me: (Thinking: from what I know of big brothers, hers might actually be more inclined to make her be the slave in the dungeon than to be her prince, and furthermore, if he had lived, she may never have been born, so instead I simply say...) "Nope."(Because it isn't, really.)

Yep, Still Surreal

February 4, 2011

I have two books in production right now.

Both manuscripts are completed aside from final proofreading. Both book covers are being designed. People who know how are typesetting and placing photographs and making words I wrote into actual real goddam book-like objects.

It's so weird, people.

The publication date for the book for Kevin is set—it's in May.

The publication date for the book for the Oregon publisher is a little loose, based on when we finish. But it's looking a lot like they will come out months, if not weeks, from one another.

Far freaking out.

Meanwhile I'm trying to learn to think like an author instead of like a wannabe author.

All that flailing around writing and throwing random stuff at the wall to see if it would stick is temporarily behind me. Some of it stuck. Now, I am razor-focused on a totally different task—marketing.

Oh, don't worry, I'm not going to get boring and normal on you. Marketing might sound straightforward, but there's still plenty of angst and fear and handwringing to be found in these waters, too.

What if no one buys my books? What if I suck at book touring? What if I say something stupid to the media? What if no media ever want to talk to me in the first place?

Stay tuned as I become wildly anxious and navel-gazey and bat-shit crazy in a WHOLE NEW WAY.

They Might Be On To Me

February 20, 2011

Chicken Little: "Mom, if you buy me this, I'll pour you a glass of beer and let you stay in the hot tub for a whole week."

I Fecking Won Something!

March 10, 2011

I won the *Oregon Quarterly* Northwest Perspectives essay contest.

I won the *Oregon Quarterly* Northwest Perspectives essay contest.

I had to write that twice because I still can't quite believe it.

(Nope! Not on LSD! I know better now, universe, ya tricky old coyote!)

Yesterday I received a very unusual phone call, especially in these days of ubiquitous electronic conversation.

"This is my favorite phone call of the year," said the magazine's editor. "You won the essay contest."

In response, I said nothing. I was too shocked.

I've entered this annual literary contest at my alma mater maybe seven times and never even been a finalist. And I won! Hot damn.

My essay is titled "The Friday's Trilogy" and it's an excerpt from the book for the Oregon publisher, which I may as well tell you now has a title: *Chance of Sun: An Oregon Memoir.*

The essay is about one of the worst periods of my life, when I bottomed out in Portland sixteen years ago. It's one of the things I had to drag out of the slammed-shut closet of the past for this book, root around in a long-ago vat of misery and try to make it into a thing of beauty.

I guess now I can say it worked. I guess now I can say I'm damn glad I tried.

Here's what the judge said:

"(I chose) 'The Friday's Trilogy,' which I found to be fresh, alive, exciting and bold writing. I had some trouble following the first few sentences, but once I was in, I was in. A compelling piece of writing, heartbreaking and redemptive. Hard to pull off without being sappy, and yet she does."

"I'll come back to earth soon," I said to the magazine's editor at the end of our conversation.

"Well, don't come back down too soon," he said. "Moments like these are too few in our world."

Things I Learned This Week

April 1, 2011

"Nothing happens, and nothing happens, and then everything happens."

—Fay Weldon

feedback

April 12, 2011

I spent a week dabbling in life as a teacher recently, on the request that I be the writer in residence at a private K-8 school. The experience was these things:

> a total blast
> very rewarding
> utterly exhausting
> fresh appreciation of every teacher, ever, anywhere

I thought motherhood was hard. Try twenty or thirty of the little beasties at once. They'll eat you for breakfast!

The second-graders were one thing. The eighth-graders were like monsters on crack. Guess I should appreciate my chickens while they are still smaller than me and haven't yet learned the powerful slow burn of a bored stare.

Yesterday, I received the evaluations from the students on the time we spent together. If nothing is better than feedback, truly nothing is better than feedback from human beings ages five through thirteen.

Some feedback highlights:

> It made me feel like a beater writer.
> Writing isn't always boring.
> I liked that there was no homework.

She seemed to really know what she was doing.

I really love how Kim came in and taught us when she could have been doing something else.

She helped us feel confident and I think she liked it.

Nothing has changed. I don't want to be a writer.

Cim wos fon. (I believe I've seen this etched onto a bathroom wall somewhere.)

And my top fave:

I thngck I am aosom ritr.

That Only Took a Decade

April 20, 2011

The doorbell just rang.

There was a box out front.

When I tore it open, I found books with my name on the front. Like, where they put the author name.

I'm not sure I believed this would ever really happen.

I am an actual goddamn author.

Yipppeee!!

Champagne and cartwheels! Taffeta and heels! A night on the town! Fame and glory!

Or, take the chickens to three-slide park, go to the grocery store, cook macaroni and cheese, fold piles of tiny socks that never seem to match, wash little bodies with tears-free soap, read *One Duck Stuck*, tuck in beautiful babies, sing *Moon River*, pour a healthy swig of vodka in a tumbler and watch an episode of *Big Love*.

Good enough.

Weird Science

April 27, 2011

Chicken Noodle: "I hate poop."

Me: "Well, it's kind of just a part of life."

CN: "I know. Animals poop and boys poop and everybody poops."

Me: "Right."

CN: "Trees poop and pee too. When leaves fall it's pee, and poop is whole branches."

Me: "Actually, the crazy truth is that trees poop gasses. Like oxygen, which we need. It's what we breathe."

CN: "*What?*"

Me: "Yeah, oxygen is tree's waste product, like our poop and pee. They get rid of something we need. That's why trees are our friends. Cool, huh?"

CN: "You mean I am breathing poop right now?"

Me: "Sure. Tree poop."

CN: "Gross! You mean that tree is pooping and peeing on me right now when we walk by?"

ME: "Yeah, kind of."

CN: "Oh, yuck! I can feel it on my arms, ugh, my legs are covered in tree poop, stop, tree, no!"

(silence...then giggling)

Me: "Chicken?"

CN: "Yeah?"

Me: "You are so awesome."

CN: "Thanks, Mom. You are too."

So. Freaking. Amazing.

May 3, 2011

Even if my writing life screeches to a halt tomorrow, I will be fulfilled. Even if I get hit by a bus tomorrow, I will die satisfied. (Audience roars with laughter. Yeah, sure she would!)

But seriously. Last night was the awards ceremony for the *Oregon Quarterly* Essay Contest. I got to read my winning essay in a fancy room on the University of Oregon campus full of literary and academic professionals, fellow winners and friends and family.

It was simply amazing.

More than my forthcoming books, even, maybe, it felt like the culmination of everything I've wanted. That essay was no spring picnic to write and it's personal as hell. It's not like reading aloud a travel story. To read my own hard-won words and have the audience respond with respect and praise was fecking awesome, I will not lie.

One audience member, who I just happened to know is a winner of a freaking National Book Award for freaking Non Fiction for freaking crying out loud, approached me after the reading and told me my essay was good. He liked it very much. He said what I did was difficult to do and that I'd done it well.

I'm going to try to put those words in my pocket and carry them with me for a while.

Because I know all of the doubt and struggle and anxiety of being a writer is still out there in front of me, no matter what I've accomplished in the past year. I know enough by now to understand there is no one final success, no single victorious finish line, just lots of little wins amidst plenty of failure and a lot of freaking hard work.

But for today, I'm going to kiss my chickens and try to hold on to the fiery glow of how it felt to stand at that mic wearing a pretty dress and the fresh flower lei my mother sent me from Hawaii and share a really pretty damn good thing I created all by myself.

Still Puzzling Over This One

May 6, 2011

Chicken Noodle: "Mom, how old is our brother today, seven? Well, I know he isn't alive, but if he were, he'd be seven, right?

Me: "Yes."

Noodle: "But where are his bones? In heaven or that place we go visit?"

Me: "His bones are in the cemetery and his soul in heaven."

Noodle: (pondering)

Me: "Do you know what a soul is? It's like your true self and your heart."

Noodle: (looks at her chest)

Me: "Not your real heart, baby. Like, the feelings in your heart."

Noodle (still pondering): "Is he going to get married before us?"

Me: "No."

Powell's Books, Baby!

June 21, 2011

For Pacific Northwest writers and authors, Powell's Books in Portland is the shiny castle on the hill. Anyone can walk in and thrall at the rooms and rooms of books. But to have your own book for sale there—that's a dream.

To actually be invited to present your book to an audience at Powell's—that's a rock and roll fantasy.

Last night, I put on a black dress, curled my hair, and stood at the Powell's podium.

The bookstore rep said the turnout was twice normal, they sold every copy of *Day Trips From Portland: Getaway Ideas for the Local Traveler* they had in the store, and they invited me back for *Chance of Sun: A Oregon Memoir*, which comes out next week (in case I failed to mention that).

Even better were the long-lost family members and friends who showed up! Way better than a high school reunion, a trip to Hawaii for Kimo, or a fortieth birthday, I'm telling you.

And guess what else? Mom is in remission.

I think I might like this book-author stuff.

However, Chicken Little is Still Unimpressed

June 25, 2011

Chicken Little: "Mom, where are you going tonight?"
Me: "To a restaurant downtown."
Little: "That's boring."
Me: "Where do you think I should go, Boo?"
Little: "London."

Make 'Em Fall Out of Their Chairs

July 25, 2011

I kicked off the launch of *Chance of Sun* at a local bookshop last night. There was a great turnout on this sunny summer evening, friends and fans and my dad and even Noodle's kindergarten teacher packing the room. Every chair, full. In the back, standing room only.

I decided to be brave and read the penultimate chapter to the crowd. The essay that won the *Oregon Quarterly* contest, the book's climax, the part of the story where I'm in danger, running wild all over Portland under the influence of a lot of tequila and cocaine and not trying very hard to stay alive.

I'd read this one at the winner's ceremony at University of Oregon and it had been an amazing experience. Here at home, in a room full of people I knew, the stakes felt higher. I mean, my dad. My kid's kindergarten teacher.

Nevertheless, I launched in, giving it my all.

The energy rose as the tension built. The audience was rapt. I was on fire. And then, at the height of the arc of the drama— SLAP—I heard a thud of something dense hitting slate.

I paused, uncertain. Had someone knocked a pile of books to the floor? Should I continue?

Then, murmurs from the back. A scuttling around. Someone summoned Captain Daddy from the audience, because the dense thing hitting slate had been someone's head. Too much migraine medicine, she said later, but for now, a call to 911. The fire station was literally across the parking lot from the bookstore, and the medics were there in minutes, which was great, since I always love seeing those guys. And they are much better at saving lives than me.

Throughout, I stood at the front clutching my past in a few sheets of paper. The audience stayed in their seats. Everyone, including me, was a bit stunned. The young woman was strapped to a gurney and wheeled out of the bookstore. The room was quiet. Still, I didn't know what to say or do. Should we just give this up, move on to the wine and crackers and book signing part?

An elfin woman with a shock of blue hair in the front row finally spoke. "Well," she said, "are you going to finish?

"Should I?" I responded tentatively.

"I want to know what happens," she said.

And so, I kept reading.

Back in the City

August 7, 2011

A decade ago, I attended my first Willamette Writer's Conference. It was one of the places my first book was kindly yet repeatedly and definitively rejected. It was also a place I learned so much, found a community of writers, and have looked forward to attending each year.

This year, right now, this weekend, I'm a teacher and presenting author at the Willamette Writer's Conference.

I guess my buddy Malcolm Gladwell was right all along. Relentless effort and persistance beyond all reason paid off.

The night before the conference opened, I had a book event in Portland. Pretty dress, reading my work, out with friends after for some cocktails. Rock and roll livin', baby. Lovin' every minute of it. Trying to enjoy the ride. Trying not to let it go to my head.

An old crusty guy approaches me in a bar. "Mind if I sit?"

I agree. He pulls up a stool, creakily climbs aboard. Small talk ensues. I learn he lives at the beach.

"How long have you lived in Newport?" I ask.

"Well, fifteen years," old crusty guy replies. "But the first seven years I was a wino. I wasn't really there. So, I've actually only lived there eight."

Right there with you, dude.

Every now and then, I have to stop and look around and realize all of this is real. I don't want to miss out on being present for the one thing I've been waiting for so long to achieve.

The Witness

August 25, 2011

Chicken Little: "Mom, remember when you crashed into that car?"
Me: "Yes, Boo, I remember."
Little: "You need to watch where you are going."

(Frustrated)
Writer-in-Residence

September 5, 2011

Two days ago, Chicken Noodle started the first grade.

Last night, she asked for some time with my computer. Having exhausted my abuse of it for the day, I obliged. After all, from what I've seen of her writing she might make better use of the thing than me.

I left her to her craft. Ten minutes of silence. Then wailing.

I returned to my office to see her crumpled in my chair, sobbing with vehemence and anger.

On the screen were these words:

The scarf
A poem
By Libby Mae Findling

A decent start. But now, tears. "The letters are wrong! I don't know what to do! What are those squiggly lines? Why does my L look that way? What if I don't know how to spell things? What will it look like when I'm done? What if no one reads it? What if no one likes it?"

Ah, the crux of it. At seven.

Insert here much writerly/motherly cajoling about how what matters is not how it looks, just getting the words down, thinking your own thoughts and recording them, I can't wait to see what you write, we'll fix the font later, Mommy will love whatever you write, I'm so proud of you, someone fix me a double vodka martini, etc.

To no consolation. She hurtled some incomprehensible existential misery at me. I left to make dinner. If it wasn't too much to bear, or too close to home, I'd have thought she was Hemingway reincarnated, and searched the desk drawers for whiskey and pistols on my way out.

Ten minutes of silence. Then wailing. I returned to the artist's space. On the screen was this:

The magic scarf
A book
By Libby Mae Findling

Modest improvements. But still. I can't do it! she sobbed. I can't! It's too hard! I want you to write it! I'm bad at this! I'll never be a writer!

I feel your pain, girlfriend. Been there. Will be there again.

At this point, I called in Captain Daddy for back up. Code 3. Patient agitated, hyperventilating. Probable anxiety attack.

He coerced her from the room with firefighter-style tough love and a healthy dose of macaroni and cheese.

After dinner, when it felt safe to venture in again:

What's your story about, Noodle?

No hesitation.

"A boy. He's going to this adventure-thing but he trips in this hole and falls into a fuzzy tree. And a baby bird falls out of its nest and he says where am I and then there's some magic stuff."

Wow. I want to read that. Stay tuned as I figure out how to nurture a first grader past a wicked case of writer's block.

Well, That Didn't Take Long

September 10, 2011

Raise your hand if you feel busy. I know, everyone is. It's the American way. Zoom around, make shit happen, talk incessantly about how you zoom around and make shit happen.

I am still book touring, I'm still freelance writing, I'm barely a published author for five minutes, and I'm already angsty about what book I will write next.

More travel? Travel with kids? Day trips? Maybe I'll write about the coast. Or eastern Oregon. Or Oregon's quirkiest places. Maybe I'll write about motherhood. Or writing. Or grief.

I promise you, whatever happens, I will not unearth the dead baby memoir. I know, for reals and for certain and finally deep in my heart, that book needs to stay burned.

Not burned like the Phoenix, not again. Burned like the Globe Theater. Like the Tuileries. Like the Gearhart Hotel. Burned, gutted, destroyed, leveled, vamoosed, never to be reborn.

Because I know now finally and forever I'm not going to cram the story of my first baby into a plot arc.

I'm never going to find that one happy ending I was searching for, because this is real life.

In real life the beginnings and endings and middles wind into one another, and around each other.

In real life, waiting for the happy ending means missing the happy middle right in front of your very own eyes.

I'm still living the story of my first baby, and my second baby, and my third baby, and I never will not be.

This is the story, right now.

It took a while for me to catch the clue, but the purpose of my first book was to lead me to the enormous gift of learning to live in today.

I will forever honor the ashes of those words for what they were: a fiery portal to the now.

And Finally, And Again, What It's All Really About

September 13, 2011

We're at the public pool. It's mayhem as usual. I sit on a grassy hill in the shade, alternately scribbling in my notebook and checking to make sure my children are still alive.

They can swim now. We've had a solid year of swim lessons. The pool is shallow. It's meant for kids. There are lifeguards everywhere.

I need not be as vigilant as so many years before. Maybe I can do some brainstorming about a next project. Maybe I can coin a phrase or two for an essay.

These small tastes of freedom are a relief, but I still don't really know how to relax. Every 100 seconds or so, my eyes scan the water. Every time I locate my chickens—even when it takes a minute—they are bobbing along together in a sea of kid heads—engaged, smiling, together.

I scribble a few words. Perhaps I will pick up the novel again. Maybe I'll write about the forest, the weather, the sea.

When I next examine the pool, I spot only Libby. Alone. She bobs tentatively.

My heart goes on alert. Nothing is wrong. But I don't so much like them apart. Have they separated on purpose? Did Maris find a pool friend? I look for her; don't find her.

Finally, my eyes pick out her little white-blonde head. She's also alone. Libby doubles back from the direction she was headed. Maris bobs in place. They don't see each other. But they are looking. They grow closer.

Warmer, warmer.

They spot each other at last.

Libby throws her arms in the air in victory. They both shriek with glee. The two girls work through the water toward each other like magnets on springs, finally and inevitably connecting.

My children throw their arms around each other and hold tight in the pool center for a good five heartbeats.

I forget all about writing and just sit still and feel happy.

THE END

ABOUT THE AUTHOR

Kim Cooper Findling is an award-winning essayist, editor and author, but not too long ago she was a stay-at-home mom trying to get her career off the ground.

Today, she is the editor of *Bend Magazine* and the publisher of Dancing Moon Press. She is the author of *The Sixth Storm*, with Libby Findling; *Day Trips to the Oregon Coast: Getaway Ideas for the Local Traveler*; *Bend, Oregon Daycations: Day Trips for Curious Families*; *Day Trips from Portland: Getaway Ideas for the Local Traveler*; and *Chance of Sun: An Oregon Memoir*. She revised the most recent editions of *Scenic Driving Oregon* and *Oregon Off the Beaten Path*.

She lives in Bend, Oregon with her husband, three teenagers, two cats and a betta fish named Romeo. See kimcooperfindling.com.